Unleashed!

T0062400

Copyright © 2009 by Bob McDermott. All Rights Reserved.

Printed in Canada. No part of this book may be reproduced in any form or by any
electronic or mechanical means, including information storage and retrieval systems,
without permission in writing from the author, except in the case of brief quotation of
passages embodied as part of a critical article or in a review.

Published by Trafford Publishing
2657 Wilfert Road
Victoria, BC V9B 5Z3
Canada

Address all inquiries to:

Bob McDermott
91-982 Ololani St
Ewa Beach, HI 96706
E-mail: Bob@UnleashedTechnologies.tv

*Scripture from the King James Version (KJV)
unless otherwise noted.*

ISBN # 978-1-4269-0428-8 (pbk)

First Printing May 2009

10 9 8 7 6 5 4 3 2 1

Your Power
Your Strength

Unleashed!

Empower Yourself
to an Extraordinary Life

*REAL LIFE EXPERIENCES
BECOME YOUR CLASSROOM THROUGH
16 INSIGHTFUL VIGNETTES*

BOB McDERMOTT

Dedicated to
Utu, the love of my life

and also

Joey, Nick, Sean, Patrick,
Matta, Brennen,
Sesilia, and Chandell

Table of Contents

Introduction

I decided to write this book because I saw a huge need for success principles from a biblical perspective. I've read many self-help books and listened to many of the self-help tapes on the market-often from new age gurus preaching about the "universe" or the "secret laws" of this or that. It's more philosophy than anything else. Two things jumped out at me. Number one, all these principles or laws (at least the useful ones) are already found in the Bible. Second, if I was going to live my life on a set of values or success principles, I wanted them to mesh with my faith in Jesus. So, I have identified these biblical principles in an easy to understand fashion.

The Bible truly does offer a road map for success and happiness. There are many authors out there today putting forth principles under some other name, but many of them are just repeating principles found in the Bible. In my opinion, two of the best Christian writers are Zig Ziglar and the late Dr. Norman Vincent Peale. Their work is rooted in biblical principles.

I have done countless hours of research on this topic and I have come up with seventeen simple principles for a successful life. You will not find a sermon in this book, but you will find principles that are reinforced with motivational quote and several scripture passages.

There is no new thought under the sun; there are no new secrets to be found. God has already laid out the road map for success for us in His Word. We often look everywhere but in the Bible for guidance. However if you focus on these biblically-based principles, I promise you will have a much better life personally, professionally, and spiritually. I can make this bold statement because these principles are not mine. They are God's.

[Principle One]
Reaping

There has been much talk in our secular culture about the "law of attraction," especially since the release of the bestselling book, **The Secret**. As Christians we should be able to see that such a theory is not supported by evidence. In order to be a law, the principle must be immutable, inflexible, and unmoving, such as the "law of gravity." The law of attraction is merely wishful thinking; it comes out of new age thinking, and a belief that somehow we are each a god. It is fatally flawed because it plays into human weakness of the flesh and greed; have everything you want with no effort; just think about it and you will attract it!

As Christians, we understand that the goodness that happens in our lives is the result of God's blessings and favor. The "secret" to reaping and sowing is having faith in God and His grace, combined with our efforts; It is knowing that He is real, using the gifts He has given us to the best of our ability with timely boldness, insight, and positive action. Reaping the harvest can only be fully enjoyed by those who have faith in our Savior, Jesus Christ.

Be not deceived; God is not mocked: for whatsoever a man soweth, that shall he also reap.

Galatians 6:7

We have all grown up hearing the biblical saying: "You will reap what you sow." Sometimes people use a rather colloquial phrase: "What goes around comes around." Have you ever really taken the time to practice this doctrine?

We have all seen televangelists asking us to plant a "seed of faith" to help their ministry and surely God will bless us. I know most people probably react cynically to such a solicitation. I used to. This is a very common reaction for people who are not Christians. However, those whose mind and heart are in the right place don't see this as a hollow gimmick. Rather, they see it as an opportunity to help others. When the preacher asks you to plant a seed, he is asking you to become a giver. He urges you to become a giver to his ministry and also to become a giver in life. You cannot receive the blessings of the Lord unless you are willing to share them and be a giver yourself.

I have shewed you all things, how that so labouring ye ought to support the weak, and to remember the words of the Lord Jesus, how he said, It is more blessed to give than to receive.
Acts 20:35

There are two types of people in this world: givers and takers. For the first forty years of my live, I was a taker. However, I did not consider myself a selfish person; I was probably your average person regarding generosity. I was just unaware that the biblical principle of reaping what you sow really works.

Years ago, I worked with a Samoan fellow named Tielu in the coffee business. I was in charge of the warehouse and distribution and this gentleman was also in charge of the warehouse. He had a very physical job. Although we didn't socialize a lot, we worked closely together and we were good friends. The fact that my wife was also Samoan strengthened our bond.

Everybody in our company liked Tielu. Although I made more money, he had a nicer car than I did and he always had extra cash in his pocket. He was always willing to loan co-workers money for lunch, a soda, or whatever they needed. If someone was in financial need, he was there to meet it. These were not large loans and he wasn't foolish with his money.

Tielu seemed to be blessed. He was by no means a rich man, but I am absolutely convinced that the Lord showed Tielu, a humble and kind man, financial favor because he was willing to share what little he had with others. He was a living example of generosity and his co-workers loved him for it.

The last time I checked on Tielu, he had retired. He had over twenty years of service with the company and earned a modest pension. Tielu moved back to his native Samoa where his modest pension made him a wealthy man in terms of the relative standard of living in that American territory.

Tielu's example has made me a more giving person at my current place of employment. I have learned that the little things count. Every time I go to lunch at a fast food place, I pick up milkshakes for both of my administrative assistants and they always appreciate it. The gesture communicates that they are valued. You cannot buy friendships or loyalty with a milkshake. However, you will build goodwill and make positive deposits in other people's emotional bank accounts. And small gestures help to create a positive, upbeat workplace.

Consider This:

● *But this I say, He which soweth sparingly shall reap also sparingly; and he which soweth bountifully shall reap also bountifully. Every man according as he purposeth in his heart, so let him give; not grudgingly, or of necessity: for God loveth a cheerful giver.*

    2 Corinthians 9:6-7

● *But he that received seed into the good ground is he that heareth the word, and understandeth it; which also beareth fruit, and bringeth forth, some an hundredfold, some sixty, some thirty.*

    Matthew 13:23

● *Sow a thought, reap an act. Sow an act, reap a habit. Sow a habit, reap a character. Sow a character, reap a destiny.*

    Charles Reade

● *Are you a cheerful giver like Tielu - one who shares and expects nothing in return, but gives for the joy of sharing God's blessings?*

I began practicing the principle of sowing and reaping in earnest after my fortieth birthday. I had a reawakening-what others might call it a midlife crisis. I was down and out and I wanted to make some changes in my life. I wanted to live differently.

This was the first time in my life that I thought about my work in a biblical sense. I began asking myself: "What is the Christian thing to do in this situation?" If I trusted in the Lord and applied this principle-not knowing what the outcome would be-how would I fair? I was about to find out.

I work for an organization called the Honolulu Council of the Navy League, whose main mission is to educate the public on the need for a strong national Sea Service-including the Navy, Marine Corps, Coast Guard, and the Merchant Marine. As I organized a fund raising dinner for the organization, I decided to take a chance and invite U.S. Senator John McCain to be our guest speaker. Most people thought I was crazy and that it was a long shot to get McCain to accept this invitation and travel to Hawaii. However, I believed that the invisible hand of God was at work.

I couched the invitation to McCain as a tribute to Joe Vasey, a retired admiral who was living in Hawaii and McCain's deceased father's best friend. Joe Vasey was a true American role model and deserved an event recognizing his lifetime of service to our country. At the age of ninety, he was in the twilight of his life. I knew that McCain would be drawn to an event like this.

In the process, I enlisted the help of two of McCain's good friends and former Vietnam POWs: retired Navy Captain Jerry Coffee and retired Marine Lt. Col. Orson Swindle-both were also good friends of retired Admiral Vasey. I was amazed to have the opportunity to work with such great Americans as Coffee and Swindle on this project. We were all bonded by the desire to recognize Admiral Vasey. These two gentlemen reminded McCain that this would be a wonderful tribute and Admiral Vasey deserved it. Thanks to their efforts, John McCain agreed to be our guest speaker.

When I got the phone confirmation from McCain's office, I immediately called Joe Vasey's daughter. I told her about how much effort had been put into this project. Joe's daughter was absolutely thrilled. She had met McCain before and knew how much McCain loved her father. We decided to keep this whole event a surprise from her father. I told her that I had gotten McCain's airfare donated by Hawaiian Air and that the lodging was going to be taken care of by the Outrigger Hotels and Resorts. She was grateful and when I hung up the phone I was ecstatic.

Then I got a call from Admiral Vasey's son-in-law, Garrett Grace and we arranged to meet for lunch. I shared my plans for the dinner with Garrett and he offered his own thoughts on the matter. Garrett and I had completely different visions on how this dinner should be handled. Our discussion became somewhat heated. I had put in so much effort on this project and it was my baby. I didn't want Garrett to take over the event and take ownership of my hard work. I told him that it was my event and we would do it my way. I left feeling like I'd put Garrett in his place.

Shortly thereafter, I got a phone call from Patrick T. Brent, a man who knew both Garrett and me. He told me that I should just give the job of coordinating the event to Garrett and that he would do a great job. "Everyone knows the hard work you have put into this, but it is a tribute to his father-in-law. The family wants to run it now," Patrick said. "Let them do it. They promise it will be first class and all you have to do is help."

I thought about it for five minutes and then called Garrett to tell him it was his baby now. I apologized for my selfishness and asked that we make a minimum amount of money for the Navy League, but other than that, it was his show. Garrett was now the event chairman and I pledged my full support to help him make the dinner a success. This turned out to be one of the best decisions I ever made.

The liberal soul shall be made fat: and he that watereth shall be watered also himself.
Proverbs 11:25

Garrett turned the dinner into a black tie event that was held outdoors under the stars at the U.S.S. Bowfin Submarine Museum (which was appropriate because McCain's father and Vasey both served aboard a submarine together). The event was a gathering of Who's Who in Honolulu. All attended to see McCain and to honor Joe Vasey. The success of the evening was a culmination of the efforts of many people with Garrett's leadership.

McCain gave a moving speech in honor of a very surprised Joe Vasey. Both Senator McCain and Admiral Vasey were visibly moved. The evening was an unmitigated success, far and above anything I could have imagined. Garrett Grace was the reason for this tremendous night of goodwill, friendship, and fellowship.

Although I spent months working on this dinner, I put aside my ego and allowed Garrett to run the whole program. In return, Garrett made me look good and helped elevate the prominence of the Navy League. He delivered in spades. I will be forever grateful to Patrick for telling me to "give" this event to Garrett.

I shared my good fortune of securing McCain as a speaker with Garrett. In return the Lord blessed me by making the night the talk of the town and by inspiring Garrett to put on a first class event that was truly spectacular. I am absolutely convinced that God blessed me for sharing this opportunity with Garrett. It gave me a chance to see the principle of reaping and sowing at work in real life. After learning that lesson, I realized the true power of God's hand if I shared and gave to others.

Consider This:

● *And God is able to make all grace abound toward you; that ye, always having all sufficiency in all things, may abound to every good work.*

   2 Corinthians 9:8

● *Happiness is not so much in having as sharing. We make a living by what we get, but we make a life by what we give.*

   Norman Macewan

● *What are you sowing today? How will you help your fellow man? Will you share a kind word with a loved one? Are you willing to plant those seeds cheerfully, and then let God create the harvest?*

We had another event and I enlisted the help of a gentleman who was not held in high regard by some people in my business world. I got to know this man well and found him to be a decent person. He had done high profile things in our community as a newscaster, radio commentator, public relations representative, and most recently, as an author. I didn't know why he had a bad rap and was seen as somewhat of a self-promoter, a person who only looked out for number one. The perceptions of him weren't true. In retrospect, I think there might have been jealously or misunderstanding.

In any case, I offered him the opportunity to be the chairman and MC for one of our dinners. It was a very visible position and I took some risk doing this because of his somewhat negative reputation. The program went smoothly. My friend did a magnificent job and quieted the naysayers and emerged as a "go to guy" for these types of events.

What was my reward? By giving this gentleman the spotlight and the opportunity to shine in front of community leaders, including the governor, the commander of the Pacific fleet, and other dignitaries, I was the recipient of a slew of "well done" comments by my board of directors. This was the most successful event in our organization's history: we netted $15,000 for charitable causes. In addition, every sailor in uniform was able to attend for free.

My motive for asking this man to get involved was based on kindness and to support him as a human being. My kindness was motivated by the invisible hand of God and he rewarded me beyond my wildest expectations. Clearly, you reap what you sow.

Consider This:

● *Be in General virtuous, and you will be happy.*

   Benjamin Franklin

● *Are you willing to trust in your fellow man and put your faith and confidence in him even when others are down on him?*

Application:

● You reap what you sow.
● You may reap what another person sows.
● God only multiplies what you have sown.
● You must weather an occasional negative harvest.
● Exploit the talents that God has given you.
● Use your talents to benefit others in a joyous fashion and you will be blessed.
● Unlike secular principles, sowing and reaping is a religious belief that requires faith-a deep faith in the power and glory of God.
● Sow positive thoughts, words, and deeds.

[The Biblical Perspective] *Reaping*

And he that reapeth receiveth wages, and gathereth fruit unto life eternal: that both he that
soweth and he that reapeth may rejoice together. And herein is that saying true, One
soweth, and another reapeth. I sent you to reap that whereon ye bestowed no labour:
other men laboured, and ye are entered into their labours.

John 4:36-38

Secularists and non-Christians often call the principle of sowing and reaping the law of reciprocity. However, long before we had ethics and particular codes of behavior, we had the Word of God. The Bible makes this principle so clear in chapter after chapter, verse after verse. I have chosen the verses above because they reinforce an often-missed point that we can reap what another man sows.

You may often reap the goodwill of an organization that you are part of simply because of the good work of those who preceded you. You may inherit money from a rich uncle and live a wealthy life. Conversely, you may reap some hardships due to the poor decisions of others. What this tells us is that we should always be sowing in a positive fashion-even if we never see the benefit personally.

How can we not think about the sacrifice that Jesus made when we think about this verse? He sowed his pain and blood on the cross so that we could reap eternal salvation. Talk about the greatest gift of all! This is the best kind of inheritance any man could ever receive and it is guaranteed to all of us. Let's follow His example by sowing seeds to benefit others.

Guest Commentary

The Golden Rule of Reaping and Sowing

by Mr. Alan Lloyd
Retired Engineer and Renowned World War II Historian

I started out as a young sales engineer selling heavy industrial equipment to sugar factories and utility companies and ended up selling electric energy to large utility customers. I was blessed with a father who was a perfect role model for his kids-a model we knew we should follow without being told. My parents provided my siblings and me with a good Christian upbringing, imbuing me with those values that I carried with me my entire life. I tried to live up to my dad's example and advice when dealing with others, particularly my customers. I found that these values served me extraordinarily well during my business career.

For example, I never ever thought of my customers as "consumers." My customers paid my salary and fed my family-there is a big difference. A wise man profits from the experience of others. I found out that "word-of-mouth" advertising is the most effective form of advertising.

As a customer advocate, I viewed my role not just as a sales engineer, but as a partner in my client's business. I wanted him to be successful; I was not in it for the quick buck, but the long haul.

About forty-five years ago, I received an order for an expensive piece of high voltage equipment. My customer said, "I want you to handle the order for the high voltage cable because I know that I won't have any problems with the cable connections and that you will charge me a fair price."

Normally, I did not handle cable orders, but I got a good quantity discount for him and I entered the order. The final billing came out fifty dollars higher than what I had quoted our customer. From my perspective, we quoted him a certain price and my quote was my word.

My integrity was on the line, not just fifty dollars (which was a lot of money in those days). I would not allow the additional charge to be passed on to my client. I insisted that the cable division stand by their original quotation and if necessary, take that extra fifty dollars out of my paycheck. The company adjusted their billing to conform to the original bid and my customer got his cable at precisely the quoted price.

On another occasion, I sold a very special stainless steel pump for a difficult pumping application to a sugar factory. Two years later, I received an order for a replacement impeller for that pump. However, before I entered the order, I phoned the customer to find out if there had been a problem. The customer said no, but it had been two years and he was getting nervous. However, because of my call, he said he would have a mechanic inspect the pump. Again, these folks were not just my customers. I was a partner in their success and I did not want them to spend money needlessly if the current equipment was working fine. I cared about them and looked out for them. Two days later, the customer called back to report that the pump was in excellent condition and requested that we cancel the order for the spare impeller. Although I lost a sale, I built up trust with my client.

I then picked up the phone and called another sugar factory that had requested bids for an identical pump. When the factory superintendent answered the phone I said, "Earl just canceled his order for a spare impeller for that stainless steel pump. The one that I sold him two years ago is still working and in excellent condition."

"Well, with that kind of an endorsement, I guess I'll have to give you the order for our new stainless steel pump," he said. It's funny how things just seem to work out when you put the interest of others first.

I had another customer who thought he should install a new power factor correcting capacitor in the sugar mill. I said that I did not think that he needed one just now and showed him why. Well the Lord must have been listening in that day, because just then the mill engineer came in to report that the underground power cable was too small to handle the extra load from the new spray pond pump.

I asked a few questions, made a quick calculation on the office black board and then told my customer that if he installed a capacitor at the spray pond, the existing cable could handle the new pumping load without difficulty. The customer gave me the order for the capacitor that afternoon. Because of my sincerity, I also got an order for a large gear reducer, which was the order that I was really hoping to get.

Throughout my career, I tried to practice the golden rule, and in every case, when I accepted an order, I believed that I was doing my customer a favor. I always tried my best to help my customers get what they really needed rather than what they thought they wanted. If I just helped them get what they really needed, my part always fell into place. In retrospect, practicing the golden rule has served my customers and me well. You do indeed reap what you sow.

[Principle Two]
Servant Leadership

Even as the Son of man came not to be ministered unto, but to minister,
and to give his life a ransom for many.

Matthew 20:28

Earvin "Magic" Johnson was a great basketball player - arguably one of the top five of all time. He was famous for how he ran the fast break and then made a spectacular pass to another player who finished with a slam-dunk. The other player got credit for the two points, but everyone in the arena knew Magic was the reason for the success of the Lakers and for that particular play. During their championship years, Magic never led the team in scoring, yet he was identified as the marquee star of the team.

Magic made others look good by his unselfish play. He was one of those rare individuals who could make those around him better. In turn, they had team harmony and they were the dominant team of the '80s. Magic was regarded as one of the greatest players of all-time because he excelled in servant leadership.

In addition, he has become a success in his life after basketball as a businessman. I have watched interviews with Magic and he still practices the same humble philosophy. He constantly gives credit to others. Whether it is his business associates or the community of underprivileged minorities he serves, Magic always practices radical humility and that is what makes him such a special person.

Magic Johnson always shared the credit, but he also did something else that was special. He took responsibility for his actions and team failures. On the court, during a fast break, if another player dropped a perfect Magic Johnson pass, Magic would often raise his hand in front of thousands of fans and say "my fault." He would take responsibility for the failed play even though everyone saw that it was his teammate who made the error.

This type of action builds goodwill and develops trust and unity. That is what great leaders do. They take responsibility for their team, organization, or company. Before you can lead, you first must know how to serve. Leadership is modeled when one puts the needs of those he leads above his own by following a calling or vision. Jesus' death and crucifixion is the ultimate example of this type of leadership.

In a much smaller sense, the father of the traditional family is supposed to lead his family through servant leadership. He may have the desire to pursue higher degrees, yet he understands that the commitment and time away from home will impact his family. The needs of the family outweigh his own desires and he lays aside his dreams until his children are older.

Putting others first is never easy. It seems to be a decreasing trend if you look at the volunteerism statistics from the Bureau of Labor. Approximately 60.8 million people "volunteered through or for an organization at least once between September 2006 and September 2007." That's a decrease by 0.5 percentage points from the previous year and 2.1 percent points from the year before that.[1]

Servant leadership should not be confused with personal servitude, which I would define as a form of slavery that rises out of some sort of obligation. On the other hand, servant leadership arises from a humble heart. The greatest leader of all time, Jesus Christ, gave his life for you and me on the cross. His

---

[1]http://www.bls.gov/news.release/volun.nr0.htm

life was the ultimate example of servant leadership.

We all work for someone else. We all have the opportunity to engage in servant leadership. The key is understanding that you are in a position to help others through your servant leadership. The president of the United States holds the most powerful position in the free world. Yet, he is there to serve us. Take away all of the trappings, pomp, and circumstance that comes with the office, and what you have is an employee who is hired by the electorate every four years. Even the most powerful corporate executives who live a life steeped in privilege are there to serve their shareholders, to increase shareholder value. Even the sole proprietor has to keep his customers happy, and on and on it goes.

Quite often, as flawed human beings, we complain and grumble about not getting enough recognition or compensation for our efforts at work. However, life would be different if we approached things the way Jesus did. He was, literally, God. Yet he came to serve, to teach, to preach the good news, and to illuminate the world. The King of kings came to us as a humble servant of his Father.

All of us want a pleasant and peaceful workplace, a setting where our hard work and contributions are acknowledged. We appreciate praise and recognition for our efforts; we want to be noticed. This desire for recognition in some form or another never goes away.

I found that the best way to "get ahead" in the workplace is to help others get what they want. In short, make your supervisor and your co-workers look good. Put their needs and desires ahead of your own. Go out of your way to help them. Be dedicated to them both individually and collectively.

If you do this in a genuine fashion, then you'll be seen as a valuable asset to your company. Not only will you benefit on a professional level, but you will become a sought after friend because people will know by your actions that you genuinely care about them. You will become their "go to guy."

This practice is not to be confused with the disingenuousness of apple-polishing or brownnosing. This principle is based on your genuine desire to make your associates successful via servant leadership. God placed us here on earth to help others as servant-leaders.

Consider This:

● *But Jesus called them to him, and saith unto them, Ye know that they which are accounted to rule over the Gentiles exercise lordship over them; and their great ones exercise authority upon them. But so shall it not be among you: but whosoever will be great among you, shall be your minister: And whosoever of you will be the chiefest, shall be servant of all.*

  Mark 10:42-44

● *The leaders who work most effectively, it seems to me, never say "I." And that's not because they have trained themselves not to say "I." They don't think "I." They think "we"; they think "team." They understand their job to be to make the team function. They accept responsibility and don't sidestep it, but "we" get the credit. This is what creates trust, what enables you to get the task done.*

  Peter Drucker

● *Do you believe that helping others is in your own best interest?*

The average Marine Corps officer is an example of the consummate servant-leader. To the uninformed, it may seem that the officers "get all the perks"... not so. In the Marines, an officer is charged with looking after and taking care of his men. When a unit is properly trained and operating at peak efficiency, then that officer gets noticed. His job is to ensure that those in his charge are fully prepared for combat in their respective roles. If he does that, he has given that young Marine the best chance of surviving hostile action.

As a supply officer with the Third Battalion, Ninth Marines, I was in charge of all the equipment, MREs, and other assets of the battalion. I was the individual charged with ensuring accurate supply counts, but my commanding officer was ultimately responsible and he took great interest in the supply account. Of course my job was to ensure that the commanding officer had a supply account that was superb. If his unit had a great account with very minor discrepancies, it would reflect on him accordingly, even though I was actually charged with the work.

This is where two biblical principles, servant leadership and responsibility, coincide. Further, if I served the commanding officer well and he received accolades for having accurate records, he rewarded me accordingly. My job was to make him shine. If I helped him get what he wanted, then I got what I wanted.

As you build trust with your boss, his confidence in you grows. However, there will come a day when you will have a new supervisor. This new person will invariably want to make some changes-improvements to the process. Change is only natural and quite healthy. In fact it is one of the main reasons that the military moves people around so often; it is good for the organization to routinely have a fresh set of eyes on the team.

That being said, we often resist change. Our egos get in the way of reason. This can stifle our servant-leadership mentality. We have a set process or methodology of doing things and all of a sudden the 'new guy' wants to change it. We instinctively reject or take offense to this because we've been doing things a certain way and it has been working just fine, thank you!

Humble yourself and try to accept the new suggestions without offense-because none is meant. Put your ego aside and embrace the new guidance. Be an example to others and lead through faithful service.

Take a moment and put yourself in the new supervisor's shoes. He is trying to do what is best for the organization by implementing his ideas. Therefore, give your supervisor the benefit of the doubt and enthusiastically implement his new changes. After all, he was hired by someone else do to this job. Help him and enable him to succeed. His success will be yours as well.

In turn, your immediate loyalty will be refreshing and you will be well on your way to developing a great working relationship. As you begin to trust and have confidence in your new supervisor, it will be reciprocated. We all know success is a team effort, so by making your boss shine, you will be noticed.

Consider This:

● *If any man serve me, let him follow me; and where I am, there shall also my servant be: if any man serve me, him will my Father honour.*

  John 12:26

● *I don't know what your destiny will be, but one thing I do know: the only ones among you who will be really happy are those who have sought and found how to serve.*

  Albert Schweitzer

● *Are you willing to put the interest of others above your own?*

As the executive director of a non-profit organization, I have responsibility for the day-to-day operations. It is my show to run. I report to a board of directors who approve of the general direction of the organization and provide oversight, but that is about it. I work closely with the president of the board because he is my de facto boss.

Early on, I made the decision to minimize my public role by putting my boss out front. We have many media opportunities and I could "hog" these for myself and use them in a selfish, self-promoting fashion (something I certainly would have done ten years ago), but I choose not to. Instead, I choose to practice servant-leadership.

I set up radio interviews for my boss. When the media asks for a quote, I always refer them to the president of our organization. This does a couple of things. First, it makes the president comfortable that I defer to him on these issues and not use the opportunities to promote my own position. Secondly, my boss sees that I am taking care and promoting him, which makes him appreciative of my goodwill gestures.

During the fundraising dinner with John McCain, I was encouraged to go onstage with McCain during the awards presentation. I refused. I said my boss belonged up there, not me. That evening was a tremendous success. I freely shared the credit with many people and I am convinced that is why it went so well. To the average person, my boss was responsible for the evening. After all, he was the Navy League president and he was the one who was onstage giving the awards away.

I helped my boss be successful and he looked great. I never knew that helping other people get what they want could be so rewarding. The president was grateful for all we had done. He acknowledged my hard work and thanked me profusely. Consequently we developed a genuine friendship because he knew I was always looking out for him and doing what was best for the organization. I helped my boss get what he wanted and he adjusted my compensation accordingly. I received a substantial increase in pay and also gained his trust. His trust was accompanied with more freedom in the workplace and a sense that we were partners in this endeavor. This was a very rewarding and liberating feeling.

And when Jesus was entered into Capernaum, there came unto him a centurion, beseeching him, and saying, Lord, my servant lieth at home sick of the palsy, grievously tormented. And Jesus saith unto him, I will come and heal him. The centurion answered and said, Lord, I am not worthy that thou shouldest come under my roof: but speak the word only, and my servant shall be healed.

Matthew 8:5-8

Here is another way to look at servant leadership. Imagine yourself as the operator of a spotlight. You could shine the light on yourself all of the time, and after awhile no one would pay attention to you. In fact you could open yourself to criticism for being self-centered. However, if you are the operator of the spotlight and you shine that light via cooperation, support, encouragement, credit, accolades, approbation, and attention on others, then you will surely be appreciated.

Servant-leadership opportunities come in all shapes and sizes. I know two elderly ladies that are still active in their respective careers. These ladies are widowed and have the wherewithal to do just about anything they want to as they move into the twilight years of their lives. They could spend their lives in leisure. Instead, they chose to devote enormous amounts of time, talents, and money supporting military families and active duty service men and women. They have no "official" government positions. They ask for nothing in return. Their efforts and hard work are legendary and precede them into any venture in which they undertake on behalf of the military.

In the course of my duties, I have been privileged to work with them on a regular basis. They are tireless workers. It became apparent to me that providing them with modest amounts of appreciation would pay huge dividends. Acknowledging their hard work motivates them to go the extra mile to help our veterans' support organization even more. In return, their increasing levels of support and continued contributions make me look good.

Jesus came as the ultimate servant. He prepared his disciples for their ministry by noting that He didn't come to be served, but rather to serve. Helping others brings the ultimate amount of satisfaction. Greatness is not defined by position, resume, or wealth, but rather by one's attitude and service to other people.

Consider This:

● *Jesus knowing that the Father had given all things into his hands, and that he was come from God, and went to God; He riseth from supper, and laid aside his garments; and took a towel, and girded himself. After that he poureth water into a basin, and began to wash the disciples' feet, and to wipe them with the towel wherewith he was girded. Then cometh he to Simon Peter: and Peter saith unto him, Lord, dost thou wash my feet?*

Jesus answered and said unto him, What I do thou knowest not now; but thou shalt know hereafter.

Peter saith unto him, Thou shalt never wash my feet. Jesus answered him, If I wash thee not, thou hast no part with me.

John 13:3-9

● *It is one of the most beautiful compensations of life, that no man can sincerely try to help another without helping himself.*

Ralph Waldo Emerson

● *Do you demand to be the center of attention, or are you willing to shine the light on others with a cheerful heart?*

Application:

● Servant-leaders should be a model of integrity.

● Servant leadership requires us to follow the example of Christ. Just as the King of kings washed His disciples' feet, we too are called to humble service.

● Servant leaders do not need a rank.

● Servant leadership is not based on a particular leadership style. Instead it is based upon a person's motivations.

● Servant leadership enables those served to reach their full potential.

● Servant leadership will propel you to the top. It works in every sphere of life.

● Practice servant leadership in all facets of your life.

[The Biblical Perspective] *Servant Leadership*

For though I be free from all men, yet have I made myself servant unto all,
that I might gain the more.

1 Corinthians 9:19

Jesus was the ultimate example of servant leadership. Paul, a follower of Jesus, was the de facto leader of early Christianity and he made the above statement of how he became a servant to everyone. His mission, as leader, was to go out and preach the good news to all who would listen. He ministered and taught at the same time. He lead people to salvation by serving them.

As the leader of the early church, Paul was often placed in humiliating and dangerous situations due to his calling to serve humankind. He could have sat back and expounded about the way to salvation. Instead he took many journeys and traveled vast distances, often in dangerous circumstances so that he could share the good news. His background made him uniquely suited to be the servant-leader of Christ's church.

We can learn many things from Paul. Even when we hold lofty positions or titles, we are here to serve others. Whether it is the president of the United States or corporate leaders, we all have a responsibility to serve humanity. This service brings great joy and among other things, makes us successful in life.

Guest Commentary

On Servant Leadership

by Roosevelt Freeman
Executive and Political Activist

Servant leadership is a term that at first glance seems contradictory. How can one be both a servant and a leader at the same time? Doesn't a leader have to be in the front and his servants in the back? Not really.

In my experience, it is possible to be both a servant and a leader. In fact, leading with the attitude of one who serves is needed to make a leader more effective and in touch with those who are being led. Leading with the mind of a servant can be a bulwark of protection against haughtiness and ultimately, a great way to crucify pride. We are told that pride is the sin that precedes the fall or failure of men.

Jesus gave us a good example of servant leadership when He washed the feet of His own disciples-men who had followed Him from one city to another as He taught and performed miracles.

It is difficult today to find someone who is both a servant and a leader. How much better would we be as husbands, wives, CEOs, assistants, politicians, and people in general if we embraced both roles? How much more integrity would our societal institutions have? Would there be fewer scandals destroying our trust in one another? I think so. After all, Jesus did it.

Putting others first is never easy.
Servant leadership arises from a humble heart.
We all have the opportunity to engage
in servant leadership. The key is understanding
that you are in a position to help others
through your servant leadership.

[Principle Three]
Responsibility

So then every one of us shall give account of himself to God.

Romans 14:12

After serving three terms as a state legislator in Hawaii, I decided to run for Congress. My political party did not support me and I lost my race to a dead opponent. I spent the next twelve months trying to get a job. I applied everywhere, including McDonald's, and no one would hire me. I was out of money and somewhat of a pariah in the community. You know what? It was my fault. I was totally responsible for my miserable condition and seeming bad luck.

When I decided to run for Congress, my party leadership made it clear that I was not their candidate of choice and that they would not support me in any meaningful way. At this point, I should have quit the race, but I decided to press on. I felt that they would come around and support me. That was my first mistake.

As months went by, my political party continued to undermine my efforts in various ways. The leadership made it clear to the media and others that I was on my own and they felt I had no chance of winning. This made my fundraising efforts almost impossible, and money is the mother's milk of politics. The party's leadership did numerous other things and all had a detrimental effect on my campaign. This made me angry and I could not ignore the insults to my ego. I lashed out and went on the attack. I tried to play "hardball" with professionals and got spanked! This was my second mistake.

I went around town and solicited money and support. People asked me why my party was not behind my effort to win. I painted a picture of woe and how unfairly I was being treated - not a very compelling picture of a future congressman or a recipe for success. That was my third mistake.

On Labor Day 2002, I was resigned to an inevitable defeat in the November general election. Then I got a phone call informing me that my opponent was dying. I was not as sensitive as I should have been, in fact I handled it horribly. I was not concerned about her or her loved ones. Instead, I tried to figure out ways I could use it to advance my own efforts. This was my fourth mistake.

Sadly, my opponent died three weeks before Election Day. However, her name remained on the ballot. I received unprecedented amounts of media coverage due to the fact that the race had such extraordinary circumstances. Voters were aware of this, but they still gave their votes to her. On Election Day, I lost to a dead person. I was a legitimate candidate. I was a sitting legislator finishing my third term. I was a former Marine Corps officer and also a Gulf War I veteran. I was a family man. I was not a granola candidate-fruit, flake, or nut. Yet, the public rejected me by a twenty percent margin and I was humbled.

However, all of my troubles could be traced back to my mistakes. I made a bad situation worse by my actions. Instead of trying to rise above it and sow positive seeds, I sowed seeds of negativity and unpleasantness.

Accepting responsibility is one of the simplest yet hardest principles to master. No one wants to admit a mistake or shortcomings; it is against our nature. It is always much easier to point to someone or something else to blame. However, this just compounds the situation and makes our dilemma even more troublesome. When others think you are trying to avoid your responsibility for a failure of any sort, they often go on the attack and exercise little charity. Humans feel - intuitively - that this is a character flaw and must be pointed out to you. On the other hand, people are very forgiving when you "fess up" to a mistake or error; they are pleased that you realize you can do better and they appreciate that gesture.

I feel the need to clarify the difference between responsibility and accountability. These two words are often used interchangeably and at times that may be appropriate.

Responsibility arises from tasks or undertakings we assume that are within our control or partial control; it can be shared among a group or individuals. For example, everyone at a McDonald's from the counter help to the president of the national corporation is responsible for the service that an individual receives when he or she orders a meal. They have even gone so far as to create a position called "Customer Care Assistant." That particular person is supposed to "establish and maintain positive communication with customers at all times and to keep the manager informed about customer satisfaction."[2]

Accountability cannot be shared. The one ultimately responsible for an issue is the one accountable. As President Harry Truman said, "You know, it's easy for the Monday morning quarterback to say what the coach should have done, after the game is over. But when the decision is up before you-and on my desk I have a motto which says 'The Buck Stops Here!'- and the decision has to be made." Truman was considered mediocre when he left office, but historians now rate him among our greatest leaders. Contrast President Truman with so many politicians today who "pass the buck" and "duck, dive, and dodge" in order to avoid any accountability.

Consider This:

● *"Why do you look at the speck of sawdust in your brother's eye and pay no attention to the*

---

[2]http://www.mcdcareers.co.uk/html/crewMember.htm

plank in your own eye? How can you say to your brother, 'Brother, let me take the speck out of your eye,' when you yourself fail to see the plank in your own eye? You hypocrite, first take the plank out of your eye, and then you will see clearly to remove the speck from your brother's eye.

Luke 6:41-43

● *The price of greatness is responsibility.*

Winston Churchill

● *Do you accept responsibility for the conditions of your life, or do you blame others for negative outcomes?*

In retrospect, things would have certainly been different if I had remained positive throughout all of the perceived slights and non-support. If I had stayed positive, people would not have had a reason to dismiss me. And maybe, just maybe, when the incumbent died, voters may have supported me, but we will never know. It took me over a year and a half to get rid of the bitterness I was carrying around in my soul. I blamed everyone, but myself. This self-induced pity kept me wallowing in a state of misery. I was in control of my own destiny the entire time. The single key to getting out of this setback was to accept responsibility for my predicament. Once I did that, my life began to change. I released all of the bitterness I had stored inside and I felt free.

Since then, I've noticed that successful people accept responsibility. I have sat in board meetings where there was some sort of problem. Several people claimed responsibility for the mistake-it almost comical. Successful people admit their mistakes and move on.

In the classic form, responsibility is the obligation to perform and is commonly associated in a workplace setting. However, responsibility encompasses all phases of life. We are responsible to lead godly lives and to also teach our family to live in a godly fashion. We can share responsibility with others. For instance, a husband and wife share responsibility for the upbringing of their family. However, each of them is accountable to God for their individual actions and efforts in this endeavor.

Personal responsibility must be a deeply held conviction; otherwise you'll be tempted to blame failures on others. You must believe that you are in some way responsible for all that has happened to you. God gives you the free will to make decisions and those decisions yield results.

When you realize that you control and are responsible for your own destiny, it is exhilarating. God blessed us with a sound reasoning process. Do the right thing, be righteous, and experience life the way God intended.

Consider This:

● *You cannot escape the responsibility of tomorrow by evading it today.*
  Abraham Lincoln

● *Does the "buck stop" with you?*

Application:

● You, and only you, are responsible for leading your life in a godly fashion.
● You may share responsibility.
● You may not share accountability.
● Practicing responsibility will enhance your sense of duty and self-worth.
● The more you are seen as responsible and accountable, the more freedom and empowerment you will receive.
● The more responsibility you assume, the more power you have.
● Help others find their sense of responsibility.
● Your responsibility toward your neighbor is of great importance.
● Everybody is your neighbor.

● Your utmost responsibility is to "love the Lord thy God with all thy heart."

[The Biblical Perspective] *Responsibility*

Jesus said unto him, Thou shalt love the Lord thy God with all thy heart, and with all thy
soul, and with all thy mind. This is the first and great commandment. And the second
is like unto it, Thou shalt love thy neighbor as thyself.
On these two commandments hang all the law and the prophets.
Matthew 22:37-40

If we live as Jesus commands, then we will have no problems with the concept of responsibility. First, we must love God with our whole heart, for He is responsible for the shower of blessings we receive each day. Go through the day with an attitude of gratefulness for the love your Father has shown you. This positive attitude will empower you; it will broaden your shoulders to carry any burden and responsibility that you may be given. With God as your undergirding, how can you fail in any of your duties?

Second, we are instructed to love our neighbor as ourselves. To put it another way, we are all in this together. This is a concept that may get lost in the hustle and bustle of life, but it shouldn't.

In Hawaii, the pace of life is a little slower than some places. Islanders tend to go out of their way to make others feel special. We call this "Aloha Spirit." The people are warm, smile more often, and helping a stranger is not unusual. Since we live on the same island, we are interdependent. We are one family.

Thus, if you live up to your responsibility to love God with all your heart, and love your neighbor, you will find that you will be able to accept and carry out greater responsibilities in life.

Guest Commentary

On Responsibility

by Sean McDermott
Student and son of Bob McDermott

Individual responsibility is on everyone's minds these days. Even those who believe that its importance has been exaggerated by the religious community accept the fact that responsibility is one of the values against which a society ought to be evaluated.

Most people have a sense of responsibility instilled in them while they are growing up-like my parents did for me. These early teachings enabled me to know the difference between right and wrong. Mom and Dad taught me that having the right to do something does not mean it is the right thing to do.

Here are a few things I've learned in regard to responsibility:

- You are responsible for what you choose to feel or think.
- You are responsible to God for the choices in your life.
- Don't blame others for your poor choices.
- You are responsible for the person you become.
- You determine how your self-esteem will develop.
- Forgive others - especially when they take responsibility for their mistakes.

Accepting responsibility
is one of the simplest
yet hardest principles to master.

[Principle Four]
Opportunities

For unto every one that hath shall be given, and he shall have abundance: but from him that
hath not shall be taken away even that which he hath.

Matthew 25:29

Recently, I received a phone call from one of our organization's big supporters. She was upset because she learned that she would not be sitting with certain people at our head table at an upcoming dinner. She was even more upset because my staff failed to inform her about this detail. She was in a tizzy and felt slighted.

This was my chance to respond properly. I took a deep breath and tried to put myself in her shoes. She was owed an explanation and a remedy. First, I clarified the problem. Then I identified the key points of the issue. I apologized for the whole mix-up and took personal responsibility for any miscommunications and failures of my staff. Then I asked her, "What exactly do you want me to do? What do I need to do to make you happy?" By asking what her specific needs were, I showed concern about how she felt. She shared her desires with me. They were all within reason and doable. I told her it would be done. I was just following biblical principles so it was very easy to remedy the situation. I was accountable and took responsibility. Next, I addressed her needs in no uncertain terms. I genuinely wanted her to feel important and to know that I cared about her desires. She ended the telephone call by thanking me profusely and even laughing about the situation. I took care of her as I would have if she were my own mother. This challenge turned into an opportunity to build goodwill and make a distraught person quite happy.

Such situations give us the chance to take what others may see as a "problem" and turn it into an opportunity to succeed. I have eliminated the word "problem" from my vocabulary. I see issues as opportunities to succeed, to excel! These are chances to demonstrate wisdom, caring, and the abilities that God gave us to "set things right." Whether at work or at home, most hurdles can be overcome with prayer, wisdom, sweat, and plain hard work.

We often complain about a particular situation instead of employing our substantial God-given powers to figure out a remedy. We need to think creatively. Take time and enter into contemplative prayer and ask God for wisdom and insight. Consider the possibilities that exist instead of focusing only on the hurdles. Look for options and solutions.

When I was serving as a Hawaii state legislator, I would routinely receive complaints about traffic issues that were clearly the jurisdiction of the City and County of Honolulu. The easy thing to do would have been to refer these people to the mayor's office. Instead of telling the complainant that this was not "my job" or area of responsibility, I took action by writing letters and making phone calls. I contacted the appropriate department head and made sure that each constituent was put in contact with the individual who could properly address his or her concerns. I followed up on the issue until the concerned citizen was satisfied with my effort. By going the extra mile, I earned citizens' respect.

Good public servants and good elected officials relish these sorts of challenges. They take a constituent complaint and turn it into a positive by working hard and paying attention to that concerned citizen. This type of service builds credibility, support, and friendships that last a lifetime and go beyond political ideology.

I once got a phone call from a mother who was angry at her children's elementary school principal. Apparently, there was a misunderstanding between both parties that was blown out of proportion. The principal was going to expel the children. Conversely, the parents wanted to sue the principal for harassment. Clearly, both parties were upset. I could have told the mother that it was beyond my area of responsibility and referred her to the state's department of education, but I did not.

I used the opportunity to be a mediator and called the mother and the principal together for a meeting. The misunderstanding was clarified and resolved. They apologized to each other. Each of them got to save face to a certain degree and I became their new best friend. Now when I see that mother or her family at the supermarket or in the community, they are still grateful to me even though I have been out of office for several years.

Consider This:

● *I can do all things through Christ which strengtheneth me.*

Philippians 4:13

● *How you think about a problem is more important than the problem itself-so always think positively.*

Dr. Norman Vincent Peal

● *When confronted with a challenge, do you point fingers, look to affix blame, or do you say, "How can I help?"*

Christopher Reeve was struck down in the prime of his life with a tragic, freak accident while riding a horse. He turned that devastating, crushing, life-changing mishap into an opportunity to increase awareness for spinal cord injury victims. Through his efforts, millions of dollars were raised to find a possible cure for this tragic affliction.

Further, he resumed his movie-making career-this time as a director. He single-handedly expanded the boundaries of what people thought a quadriplegic could accomplish. He was politically active and he used his disability to help others. He had a more positive and greater impact on the world after his accident than before it. Christopher Reeve is truly someone who took lemons and turned them into lemonade.

Nordstrom is a store that is famous for going above and beyond the call of duty to make customers happy. Nordstrom built a store in Alaska at a location that had previously included a tire store. A customer, unaware that the tire store no longer existed, brought a tire into Nordstrom and asked for a refund and the refund was issued. This is consistent with Nordstrom's customer-first approach to business. They are known for sending "thank you" cards to customers and for hand-delivering orders to the home of customers. They don't require a receipt when customers return merchandise that is known to come from their store.[3] They do everything they can to take advantage of opportunities to please customers.

One day I made a huge blunder at work. We have an exclusive membership category that costs $500 per year just for the privilege of joining. All of the "movers and shakers" in town are members of this group. One day when I was in a rush, I needed to alert this group to an upcoming event. In the process of sending out an e-mail blast, I mistakenly attached the membership roster to the electronic message. It would not have been so bad if the roster had not contained credit card numbers and security codes. This was not an act of malice, just an honest mistake.

As you can imagine, the thoughts of identity theft ran through everyone's head. No one felt worse about it than I did. I knew that the impact of this mistake would not be over in a day and I would have to settle in and accept

[3]http://www.snopes.com/business/consumer/nordstrom.asp

the anger from the people I put at risk. I was distraught and overwhelmed with a feeling of helplessness. Could I get fired over this episode? How would people view me? I needed help.

I sat down at my desk and prayed. After a few minutes, the Lord took away my feelings of uncertainty and fear. I thought about what I could do to fix the situation and I what I could learn from my mistake. I learned more about the character of the people I dealt with. I had some unexpected supporters. The board members that I thought would be the first to call for my head were supportive. There were others that I had always showed respect and kindness now wanted me fired.

From a practical standpoint, I learned that our information control was non-existent and it had to change. I immediately took corrective action and erased all personal credit card numbers from my files. I sent a personal letter of apology to each member, providing information that would help them thwart identity theft. I did this with the guidance and support from my board president and vice president. These two gentlemen stood by me and helped me through this tough time. With their help, I was able to put a plan of action into place that showed our members that we were taking corrective measures and took this breach seriously. It demonstrated that I was deeply sorry and concerned for any pain or inconvenience I might have caused them.

A result of the corrective action was that we received compliments on the way the whole situation was handled. We revamped our information controls and implemented some long overdue controls. More importantly, we demonstrated care, concern, and goodwill towards those whom I put at jeopardy.

Consider This:

● *Get wisdom, get understanding: forget it not; neither decline from the words of my mouth.*
Proverbs 4:5

● *Every adversity, every failure, every heartache carries with it the seed of an equal or greater benefit.*

    Napoleon Hill

● *We have two choices when confronted with our mistakes. We can dwell in misery and hold a pity party or we can ask the Lord for strength and guidance to make the best of the situation. How do you normally respond?*

Whenever presented with a major challenge or problem, take the time to pray and focus on the issue. You will be pleasantly surprised to find that God will supply you with choices and wisdom. It may sound a little simplistic, but here are a few examples of positives growing out of negatives: The mother who grieved the death of a loved one started M.A.D.D. - Mothers Against Drunk Driving; the smoker who wants to quit and takes up exercising; the community that has a drug-ridden park and decides to start a midnight basketball program to rid the park of undesirables and to reclaim the park.

Life is not always going to go as planned. You have heard the old saying, "If you want to make God laugh, make plans." This is not to say we should not have goals, hopes, dreams, and desires - we should! But we must also understand that God sometimes changes our circumstance or gives us obstacles as lessons to learn from. From God's perspective there are no accidents. Everything happens for a reason. We must have faith and trust that He has our best interests in mind.

Application:

● Clarify the challenge. Identify the root cause and take positive action.

● Tragic events happen. If you find yourself in such a situation, pray about it and then look for opportunities to act.

● Negative consequences sometimes occur as a direct result of our decisions.

Be accountable and learn from the situation.

- No matter what challenges or constraints come your way, you can always do something positive.
- We cannot always control what comes our way, but we can control how we react.
- Use challenges to learn and teach others by your actions and deeds.
- Always look at the bright side of things.
- Be an irrepressible optimist.
- After prayer, take decisive action. Do it now!
- View all challenges with a Christ-imbued spirit.
- The opportunity you are looking for may be right in front of you.

[The Biblical Perspective] *Opportunities*

For they that are after the flesh do mind the things of the flesh; but they that are after the Spirit the things of the Spirit. For to be carnally minded is death; but to be spiritually minded is life and peace.

Romans 8:5-6

When we talk about opportunities, we must first focus on the greatest opportunity that we all have right in front of us-that is to take full advantage of the salvation available through the death and resurrection of Jesus Christ on the cross. If you do this, then you have taken the most important step in living a godly life here on earth. A godly life equals success.

Too often, when confronted with earthly problems, we get depressed due to the circumstances. When viewed in the flesh or the natural, these problems can become overwhelming. However, when viewed with a spirit imbued with Christ, these problems can be viewed as challenges that offer each of us an opportunity to use our God-given gifts and Christ-filled spirit to find a solution to the challenge. Viewed in this fashion, we have the opportunity to make things better-an opportunity to "shine."

With a Christ-filled Spirit, challenges become opportunities. No challenge is too big or small when you are walking with God. Seize opportunities each day and glorify God by using the gifts He has given you.

Guest Commentary

On Opportunities

by Kevin Moore
Elected Official, Realtor, Eternal Optimist

"It is like the mustard seed that, when it is sown in the ground, is the smallest of all seeds on earth. But once it is sown, it springs up and becomes the largest of all plants..."

From a young age, God has gifted me to see the things that can make a community better, long before they are built. Children are like scriptural mustard seeds because they need sunshine, recreation, and love to grow into better human adults. They start small and with the right nutrients; they can become great.

Looking back on my youth growing up in Santa Clara, the best times were when I felt close to God in nature. I witnessed the benefits of a city that focused on young people and that was known as the youth sports capital of the world when I was a boy. As I went through my twenties and thirties, I knew somebody had to step up to claim the tradition of putting youth first for another generation. The downside of Silicon Valley is that we paved over hundreds of acres of orchards, but we often forgot to plan for the health of tomorrow's kids.

Though Santa Clara still had a world-class international swimming facility, we needed new opportunities to give young people options so they could maintain the healthy lifestyle they need to thrive. A community can find opportunities where people too often find insurmountable challenges. There is no excuse not to get outside and get healthy. I learned through my early public service that most great projects happen because a few visionaries are willing to put their dreams into action.

With the demographics changing in our part of California, we found that thousands of young Santa Clarans wanted to play soccer. So I launched the concept of building a world-class youth soccer facility. Newspaper journalists bashed the idea as impractical and some community leaders figured it would be too difficult to make a reality, but I was never more confident that our kids really could come first. Even our board voted to disband, but I did not give up and I simply reformed a new steering committee. One cannot stop an idea whose time has come! Now Santa Clara has an internationally renowned soccer complex with three outstanding fields for our local youth. My reward is watching young players enjoy their game each weekend.

As a child, I also used to ride my bike through the streets of town, back before we became such a busy city. Over time kids could no longer ride their bikes safely on our increasingly busy streets. I realized we could develop a creek trail path to connect schools, parks, and other city facilities. In the 1970s, the city abandoned its creek master plan and when I brought it back up in the 1990s, people laughed. However, we have now rejuvenated our creek side so our young people can spend time outdoors biking, walking, and relaxing.

Santa Clara is close to landing the five-time world champion San Francisco 49ers football team as it searches for a new hometown. Years before I was elected to the city council, I sent a letter to the 49ers administration, encouraging them to look at Santa Clara as an option. I figured that if I was elected to the city council I would probably be taken more seriously. So, I ran and won. And, now we are at the brink of bringing the 49ers to the best stadium complex in the West. The resources this team will bring will revitalize many parts of town and will complement the soccer facility and the creek trail, which, coincidentally, border the parcel where the stadium will be built.

Like a mustard seed, anyone can take an idea to reality, with faith, hope, and a never say die attitude. This never-say-die attitude is a gift from God. My recommendation is to unwrap the gift.

[Principle Five]
Language

Keep your tongue from evil and your lips from speaking lies.

Psalm 34:13

You don't need to look hard to find statistics regarding how acceptable the practice of lying has become. One study revealed that fourteen percent of professionals admit to lying on their resume. Another twenty percent say they "fudged a few things," but they didn't consider such practices to be a lie.[4] According to another study, four out of five people admit to hiding purchases from their significant other.[5] And yet another study revealed that one third of the respondents were so suspicious about their partner that they went through their significant other's email and text messages to see if they could catch them in a lie.[6]

I know a man who has a tendency to embellish the truth under even under the most normal of circumstances. He is not a particularly talkative individual. He will not normally go out of his way to strike up a conversation. However, given the opportunity to embellish his dialogue, he will take advantage of unwitting or unknowing individuals with fantastic tales of fancy.

This disorder is particularly troubling when he gets drunk. That is when the whoppers really start to flow. He knows no reasonable limit to even

---

[4]http://hr.blr.com/news.aspx?id=3359
[5]http://money.cnn.com/2008/06/02/pf/spouse_money.moneymag/
[6]http://www.topnews.in/health/one-five-brit-men-admit-paying-sex-survey-2366

disguise his fairy tales. He lies about his golf scores, telling people that he scores well under par on a regular basis. He even goes so far as to say that he has golfed with Tiger Woods and that he often wins local and PGA tournaments. To the unknowing, non-golfer, this seems impressive at first, but after some time, his stories don't add up.

Lying damages an individual's integrity and eventually destroys it. I have seen it happen to my friend. He is no longer held in high regard. People have lost respect for him. He is no longer invited to family get-togethers. Sadly, he has earned the reputation of being an empty "tin-can;" he makes a lot of noise but he's empty inside. He does not have anything of substance to say. I don't know why he continues to exaggerate wildly. He now reaps what he has sown. He speaks like a fool and is treated as a fool.

Aside from the personal damage he has done to himself, the damage he has exposed his children to is a tragedy. His two youngest sons have adopted his habit of lying. It seems they want to sound a little more impressive. I have observed their behavior and it is scary. These young men don't know the difference between fantasy and reality because they were never taught to attach negative consequence to their lying. They both lie so well that you begin to doubt yourself. When you question them on details that they clearly can't answer, they become even more insistent.

I had the occasion to witness one of these young men being questioned by a lawyer on a legal matter. It was a family dispute and he was clearly lying. Yet the attorney went back and questioned the other party in the matter in private chambers because this gentleman was so believable in his prevarications.

Consider This:

● *May the LORD cut off all flattering lips and every boastful tongue.*
   Psalm 12:3

● *The general message of the neighborhood is that the truth is best. If we can share ourselves with our kids in ways that aren't frightening to them, that's the greatest gift we can give anyone - the gift of an honest self.*

Fred Rogers, Mr. Rogers Neighborhood

● *Do you practice truthfulness and honesty in all situations or do you tell 'little white lies' on occasion to ease your own personal discomfort regarding a particular issue?*

When I worked in the supply office of the Third Battalion, Ninth Marines during the first Gulf War, I saw another example of how damaging negative words can be when one individual's words became a cancer in our unit.

Our unit was among the first deployed to thwart Saddam Hussein's military threat. We were stationed on the border of Northern Saudi Arabia and were often referred to ourselves as a "speed bump" because we were relatively unprotected as a lone infantry battalion placed in a forward position. Across the border in Kuwait were some 400,000 Iraqi soldiers. The days of waiting stretched into months. Most nights the junior officers would gather on a big sand berm in front of the command post where guys went to chew the fat. The battalion commander was a lieutenant colonel. He was not supposed to fraternize with his junior officers and consequently he did not come out to the berm.

Our discussion was often topical and sometimes turned into a grumbling session. The catalyst for this negativity was a chemical protection officer who believed the battalion commander did not take his training seriously enough; the chemical protection officer felt disrespected and consequently had an ax to grind. He became the commanding officer's biggest enemy and spreader of verbal poison. This went on for about two months. Eventually it led to an all out revolt against the battalion commander. All of the company commanders went to see the regimental commanding officer and said they could not follow the battalion commander into combat. The regimental commander was forced to make a tough decision. He could get rid of the mutineers and disloyal officers or replace the battalion commander. Neither was a good choice. He made the tough call and replaced the battalion commander, whose career as a Marine officer was effectively over.

In retrospect, the battalion commander was poorly served by his staff. There was a cancer in the unit and it needed to be excised. It didn't happen and it led to an unfortunate consequence. No one was happy and a good man's career was destroyed. I felt terrible about what happened. Once he was reassigned, I visited him and shared some kind words with him. It brought him to tears.

Consider This:

● *The glue that holds all relationships together-including the relationship between the leader and the led is trust, and trust is based on integrity.*

Brian Tracy

● *When communicating, do you use positive words, or negative words? Are you a builder or destroyer?*

Positive words are like flowers that bloom. Have you ever had someone come up to you and say that he has heard really good things about you? What a wonderful experience. However, be cautious of people who offer flattery - less than genuine compliments. They are trying to curry favor with you for some reason or another. They know the power of words and thus are trying to sway you. Positive comments and outright flattery can be intoxicating. Just like when a young man is courting a young lady, he might just say and do anything to win her favor.

In the business world, car salesmen go out of their way to be nice and show interest in a new customer. Studies show that once a potential customer leaves the lot, he will not come back. So the salesman has one chance and one chance only to close the deal. It is an art and a science; he will show interest in you and compliment you on your attire, selection of vehicle, etc.

In your personal life, develop a habit of deflecting compliments. When a supervisor thanks you for a job well done-politely accept his kind words, but immediately remind him (and yourself) that it was a team effort and the entire organization deserves the credit. This prevents you from taking any one's comments too seriously. Your value or measure as a person should not be based on what other people say about you, good or bad.

If you use positive language and refrain from negative utterances, you have a positive impact on your community and the world. Good words and thoughts miraculously attract other good words and thoughts. Positive comments and rhetoric are self-fulfilling prophecies. If it is God's will, you will become what you think, speak, and pray about. When you continue to dwell on good things and positive thoughts, this is what your life becomes. Your spirit becomes more in tune with God's.

Early on, when I was starting in politics I would often write letters to the editor or op-ed pages for the local newspaper. I did this to become involved in the public policy discussions of the day and to advance my career as a politician. I often noticed other pieces would be critical of the status quo or of a public policy issue. Along the way I have found three things to be certain: 1) Our daily media prints far too much negatively. 2) It is much easier to criticize and find fault with something or someone than it is to be positive. 3) The media is thirsting for and will print just about any positive commentary.

As an individual who wants to be more Christ-like, I look for the good in things. When I submit an article or commentary, it is positive and therefore it gets printed the next day. I mean it works like magic! No kidding. Be positive and you move to the front of the line while all the complainers and whiners are sent to the end. Positive words with positive intentions are expressions of God's love-that is why they are effective and powerful.

Sometimes I am surprised at how reckless people are with their language. Positive, caring, and loving words can provide encouragement when someone is down or sick. We say these positive things because we instinctively know that these utterances will make the person feel better.

Negative words seem to have just as much power as positive words-even more perhaps because they hurt so much. We tend to dwell on them and as we get older negative words carry more power. But here is a secret about negative words: they can't continue to hurt you if you forgive the person who said them. Forgiveness allows the pain to drain away. It is like the sweet fragrance that remains after a flower has been crushed.

If you fail to forgive the offender, then his or her negative words continue to have control over you because you are still carrying their negative effects around inside you. If it is too uncomfortable to forgive the offender in person, say a prayer for that person. You will discover that prayer for forgiveness has enormous power.

When people ask me if I like my job, I respond enthusiastically. It is an absolute blessing to work with the people I do. It is the good people created in God's image, who allow me to enjoy my work. I can't fully express how happy I am at my current place of employment. My boss is the finest man I have ever known-a gentleman to the tenth degree. He has the patience of Job and the wisdom of Solomon. I am blessed to work for him. I am fortunate to learn from him, an education that has proven invaluable.

I'm blessed with a supportive staff and I also support them. Look at your situation in a positive fashion and count the blessings God has given you; it will make your job much more enjoyable. To quote Dr. Wayne Dyer, "If you change the way you look at things, the things you look at change." When people ask me, "How are you?" I reply, "I am outstanding, but I'll get better."

Tap into the Spirit of God and use language that is empowering. This will make you more effective and happier in every endeavor or challenge you undertake. You will see a remarkable change in those around you, and more importantly, yourself. Positive words, thoughts, and prayers equal a positive outcome in line with God's will for you.

Consider This:

● *Few things in the world are more powerful than a positive push. A smile. A word of optimism and hope. And you can do it when things are tough.*

   Richard M. DeVos

● *Try using a positive vocabulary for one day. See what a difference it can make. Are you willing to use words that bring life rather than death?*

Application:

● Use positive, uplifting words.
● Use positive words to describe a negative situation; it will not seem so bad.
● Positive words help avoid confrontation, misinterpretation, and anger.
● Positive language enables you to project a positive self-image.
● Positive language builds trust and friendship with family members and co-workers.
● Eliminate negative words and phrasing from your vocabulary that might be interpreted as sarcastic or patronizing.
● Freely distribute genuine verbal "pats on the back," especially to co-workers, family, and friends.
● Chose your words carefully. Once you say something, you cannot "un-say" it.
● Listen attentively.
● Read books that reinforce the importance of a positive attitude.
● Be positive right now!

[The Biblical Perspective] *Language*

Cease, my son, to hear the instruction that causeth to err from the words of knowledge.

Proverbs 19:27

In this chapter, I talked about the power of language-the power of the spoken word and how it can hurt or heal. The other end of the spectrum is listening. If no one listens to what is being said, then there is no point is saying anything.

In the verse above, the Lord states plainly that if you stop listening, you will stop learning. Too often, we hear someone speaking, but we do not really digest his or her message because we are not listening. Consequently we can't learn anything from what that person is saying. It has been said that the use of words only make up about twenty percent of the communication process; the rest is vocal intonation, body language, and pace of the dialogue. To pick up these pieces of communication you must focus and seek to understand; not just hear.

Here's a good way to tell whether you've been listening or not: ask yourself whether you can repeat the gist of everything you've just heard somebody say. If you can, then you are on the right track and you'll be much more successful in dealing with that person. The same principle applies to all relationships.

God, in His infinite wisdom, knows how important listening is - that's why He gave us two ears and one mouth. So use them accordingly and in proportion.

Guest Commentary

The Power and Essence of Language: A Samoan Perspective
by Eni F.H. Faleomavaega

"E pala le ma'a ae le pala le tala"
Samoan proverb: Rocks and stones will decay, but words will not.

Upu in the Samoan language is translated as "word(s)" in English. A combination of upu makes a tala or statement. Tactful arrangements and clever usage of words give the Samoan language wisdom, character, class, and above all, power.

There is nothing better that can reflect the power and essence of words in Samoan tradition and language than the above proverb. It reveals the basis of Samoan life-words have a deeper, indestructible dimension that gives Samoans the ageless meaning of life and what Samoan existence is all about.

Without going into anthropological theories, one can simply say that Samoa has been an oral society for thousands of years. All communication was by word of mouth; and every word, phrase, and saying had special meanings. Generation after generation passed them on and thereby perpetuated the traditional way of life from the beginning. These set patterns of disciplined practices are the guidelines on which Samoans live their daily lives from season to season, year to year, and generation to generation. These are the foundations for both the young and the elderly-a foundation that is cast and molded with words, something stronger than rocks and stones.

The Samoan language is powerful because it has stood the test of time. The most amazing fact is that even after all these years the language is still serving its purpose by accommodating and carrying that fa'asamoa or the Samoan way of doing things.

The Samoan language has been the identifying factor of all Samoans in the past and present, because it is the common thread that connects families, villages, communities, and the people culturally. Every Samoan word relates to the culture's existence, and every phrase and saying provides meaning to a way of life that is now being challenged by outside influences and modern Western technological advancements.

We have lost more words than we have gained over the years. Various changes have been imposed and they have altered traditions and the Samoan culture from what it was twenty, fifty, or even a hundred years ago.

Perhaps the most positive changes came about when missionaries Christianized the islands in the late seventeenth century-when most of what were considered "pagan" practices were ultimately banned. This was also when the language shifted from an oral tradition to a written language because Samoans were taught how to read and write. The Lord not only blessed the Samoans with salvation through his son Jesus Christ, but he gave us the written "Word."

With modernization, a simple glance at the dictionaries compiled by the early westerners in Samoa in the late 1800s would reveal many words that are rarely used in daily Samoan conversation now. It is rather sad that these words no longer have any meaning since what they initially represented and stood for are of no use. Nevertheless, they stand for a time in history that we can still learn from-a time that still gives meaning to the future of the Samoan people.

How often does one hear Samoans emphasizing what "people are saying" (tala a tagata) or "assault/punish verbally" (fasi i upu ma tala)? How often do we have major disputes, conflicts, and extreme difficulties settled by just simple exchanges of soft-spoken words and traditional oratory to resolve the problems?

The power of words in the Samoan language is limitless and such power often becomes spiritual in that it heals personal and communal differences, and provides peace and harmony out of chaos and anarchy.

I am reminded of John 1:1, which states, "In the beginning was the Word, and the Word was with God, and the Word was God." Samoans, in their simple way of viewing life, see words as the vitality of life-the whole meaning of existence. Rocks and stones will decay, but words will not, especially the Word of God.

Perhaps this is why Samoans are so obstinate in their usage of the words upu and tala. Upu a le Atua (Word of God); tasi le upu (one word, to be used for disciplinary purposes); 'ai upu or 'ai tala (which literally means to eat or consume too many words or statements-used against someone who is highly antagonistic or disobedient). Then there is my favorite saying: O tama a tagata e fafaga i upu, o tama a manu e fafaga i fuga o la'au, which translates to: The children of men are fed by words, but young animals are fed by leaves of the trees. The whole essence of Samoan living is guided by the use of language and the Christian faith.

While others may disagree, I submit that the monumental task of translating the Holy Bible into the Samoan language was perhaps the most important development in transitioning a society from its oral traditions to that of a written one. The early missionaries who followed Reverend John Williams first introduced Christianity in Samoa in 1830 by devising an alphabet based upon phonetic sounds of Samoan words. In essence, this is what makes Samoans slightly above the animals, and a little below the angels.

... use positive language
and refrain from
negative utterances ...

[Principle Six]
Patience

Better is the end of a thing than the beginning thereof: and the patient
in spirit is better than the proud in spirit.

Ecclesiastes 7:8

Patience is an extraordinarily important, yet underrated principle for success. Patience doesn't come naturally. All you need to do is hit the road on the way to work each day to know what I'm talking about. Fifty-nine percent of workers surveyed by CareerBuilder.com say that they experience road rage. Ten percent say that they "usually or always" experience road rage.[7]

I have learned a lot about the virtue of patience over the last several years. My boss gave me a lesson in patience once when we had a problem at work. His cool head and reasoning steered us through a very rocky set of circumstances; it is no coincidence that he is a regular church-going man.

Our treasurer had not filed our tax returns with the IRS for over three years. I was relatively new to the organization and found out about this issue because I asked our treasurer "Sally," for a tax clearance form to collect an awarded grant. Rather than handing me the form, Sally attacked the substance of the grant and my authority to pursue it in the first place.

She e-mailed my boss and criticized my leadership style and the way I was running the organization. I talked to her and she seemed unreasonable to me.

[3]http://www.consumeraffairs.com/news04/2006/10/road_rage_study.html

I could not understand why she was going after me. This went back and forth for a few days. Finally, my boss, the vice president, Sally, and I had a meeting to talk about the grant, but Sally directed the discussion once again to the subject of my leadership abilities and judgment. Sally was smart and kept us on our heels. She even accused me of letting my wife sign company checks and other financial malfeasance. I got so angry I had to get up and leave the office to cool down. When I returned, they were still discussing my leadership style and abilities. Needless to say, I was not pleased with the way the discussion was going. We were supposed to be talking about the grant and the filing of our taxes.

Eventually we got around to discussing the delinquent tax returns and why they had not been filed. She claimed that the offices' record keeping was dubious at best and the financial figures were very troubling to her, and therefore she had never filed the returns. In my opinion, her explanation did not pass muster and she was putting our organization in jeopardy. My boss asked her to provide a timetable when she would have the taxes filed. She refused to give a date. My boss offered to hire an outside firm if she was unable to find the time, but she declined the offer. Then he offered to hire part-time help for her and again she refused. Finally, he offered to pay her for her time if she would just expedite the matter.

After about an hour of going back and forth, she finally gave us a date-she said she would need one month to complete them. The month came and went. She gave us another date, and again she missed her own mark. She missed a third mark. Nearly four months had passed since I first learned out about our non-compliance with the IRS filing requirements. As she missed each deadline, I became more and more frustrated. I begged my boss to fire her. He said, "No Bob, we are going to ride this one out to the end." I could not understand his reasoning. She was hurting our organization. She was also still on the attack. When asked why she didn't have the books in order, she blamed the allegedly bogus numbers that were presented in years past. She kept attacking and staying on the offensive. I had long since decided to keep my mouth shut and let my boss deal with her. I took myself out of the equation so it was no longer a personal issue.

After she missed her third deadline, my bosses hired a CPA firm to come in and prepare the taxes and they finished the job in three days. We filed and ended up with over $20,000 in fines for filing late.

When we alerted Sally that we had hired a CPA firm, she was livid. She made all sorts of threats and accusations, not against me anymore, but against anyone who was involved in bringing our books into compliance. She spread her accusations through e-mail citing "accounting improprieties and erroneous figures." She said she would not stand for this and was going to report us to the state authorities. What a nightmare! She repeated these accusations at our board meetings. A special committee of past board presidents was set up so she could discuss her issues. She talked and talked and talked, but never offered any substance to her allegations. She realized that a good offense was her best defense. She just kept pointing fingers.

My boss waited Sally out. My boss was right in letting her continue to blow off steam until there was no steam left. That's not to say that my boss was not afraid that Sally would cause trouble for us by making her unfounded allegations public. As a non-profit organization, all we have is our name and goodwill. However, my boss saved us from any public embarrassment by exercising patience in the ordeal.

In the end, she talked herself off the board due to lack of credibility and finally left on her own. She embarrassed herself and could no longer show her face around our organization. No word of this mess was made public and we recovered. I would not have waited as long as my boss did. I would have taken action much sooner. The likely result would have been less favorable than the final outcome my boss attained. He was patience personified.

Patience is a virtue. Every successful person knows that good things come to those that wait. Patient leaders move forward in an expeditious fashion once they have made a decision on a particular issue, but they also exercise good judgment by doing their due diligence; research, contemplation, and prayer. After some reflective thought, they then take action and wait for the results. The process reminds me of the principle in which God turns an acorn seed into a mighty oak. God plants the tiny acorn seed. Over time, he nurtures the seed-providing water, light, and nutrients. No one can rush the process. No amount of wishful thinking or fretting will speed up the growth of the seed. However, with time and patience, the seed turns into a beautiful oak.

Consider This:

● *Strengthened with all might, according to his glorious power, unto all patience and long suffering with joyfulness; Giving thanks unto the Father, which hath made us meet to be partakers of the inheritance of the saints in light...*

  Colossians 1:11-12

● *Patience and perseverance have a magical effect before which difficulties disappear and obstacles vanish.*

  John Quincy Adams

● *How would you have handled the situation I was in? Would you have proceeded in a deliberate cautious fashion putting your trust in God, or would you have been like me, quick to act and impatient?*

Ronald Reagan was another man who exhibited great patience. He wanted to run for president in 1968, but he waited. Then in 1976 he challenged the sitting vice president, Gerald Ford, and ran for the Republican nomination. He came close, but was frozen out by party bosses who thought he was too conservative. Many would have been bitter with what happened to him in 1976, but not Reagan. He continued to speak and write and ran again in 1980. He finally won the Republican nomination and then he won the presidency of the United States in 1981.

Reagan persevered with patience and it paid off. All the while, he kept a positive attitude and this Christian man believed that he would eventually have a good outcome.

His patience was displayed with his political adversaries and other endeavors. Whether it was Congress or the Soviet Union, he always kept his eyes on the prize and worked toward his final objective with patience. He got his tax cuts through Congress with patience and charm. Many of the media pundits made fun of his economic policies, especially when the economy was faltering two years into his presidency. However, by the time he was re-elected in 1984, his economic policies had taken affect and America was booming. Reagan was patient with his policies and America rewarded him with a landslide re-election.

Reagan won the cold war with patience and determination. When many of the chattering class ridiculed him as a buffoon and a simpleton, he stuck to his beliefs and they paid off. He has since gone on to become one of the greatest presidents in our history. He finally got his due.

Consider This:

● *Be patient therefore, brethren, unto the coming of the Lord. Behold, the husbandman waiteth for the precious fruit of the earth, and hath long patience for it, until he receive the early and latter rain.*

James 5:7

● *He that can have patience, can have what he will.*

Benjamin Franklin

● *If you had been Ronald Reagan, what would you have done after the 1976 election? Would you have changed course to mollify your critics?*

Let me share you one final example of patience. From the moment I was hired to be the executive director of the Navy League, it was clear that one of our board members "Betty" did not like me. During my first two years at the organization Betty criticized me, no matter what I did. It wasn't constructive criticism. Instead it was nitpicking, useless, and debasing.

In hindsight, I can see why. Betty was a smart, driven-career woman who was successful in the business world. She was a real go-getter. At the age of 47, this relatively attractive lady had no husband, children, or family in her life. She was also very liberal.

I am the exact opposite of Betty. I am an old fashioned guy with 1950s values, a throwback to another time. The most important thing in my life is taking care of my family. My heroes are John Wayne and Ronald Reagan. I am a former Marine Corps officer. I am a walking poster boy for political incorrectness.

Since it was clear that Betty was no fan of mine, I went out of my way to try to make peace with her, but to no avail. She continued her negativity and her constant put down of my performance to other board members. I know this because others on the board told me so. This situation caused me some emotional pain. On a personal level, I liked Betty. I thought she was smart and a good contributor to our mission and organization.

Finally, after several months of this nonsense, I invited Betty out for a cup of coffee so we could talk about our different approaches and management philosophies. I wanted to improve communication, work together, and move forward. Over the course of two months, I asked Betty for a meeting on three separate occasions. Despite the fact that I made the invitation open-ended, she was always too busy.

My boss watched as this saga played out. The end of my efforts to reach out came one year during the Christmas season. I sent Christmas cards to every board member before our December meeting. I know they all got them because they all thanked me. I took special care in selecting Betty's card because she was Jewish; therefore I gave her a card wishing her a blessed Chanukah celebration. I made sure that I spelled everything correctly so that I didn't offend her with the card.

After the Christmas meeting was over, I had to leave immediately. Betty stayed behind and bad-mouthed me to various board members. Another female on the board called me and said, "Watch your back. Betty is at it again." This was the last straw. I told my boss, the board president, that I had done everything in my power and was not going to waste my time on trying to improve the situation. He understood and I was relieved.

I no longer cared what Betty had to say about me. I continued about my business, doing the best I could with my nose to the grindstone. Betty's negative comments were not in sync with the positive things that were happening in the organization. There was a clear disconnect. I just had to be patient and hope that either Betty would warm up to me or that she would leave the organization. I really hoped we could find some common ground and continued to exercise patience in hopes that the situation would resolve itself in due course-in God's timing, not mine.

It became clear to the incoming board president that she was a negative influence to the Navy League. Betty was not reappointed to the board and "lost face." She was a smart, talented woman, yet her negativity cost her a position that she really wanted to keep.

Patience is an extraordinarily important, yet underrated principle for success.

Consider This:

● Patience and fortitude conquer all things.

   Ralph Waldo Emerson

● Slow and steady wins the race.

   Aesop

● Patience is the companion of Wisdom.

   St. Augustine

● *Do you have the faith and patience to ride out life's little bumps and slights?*

Application:

● Practice patience when something disagreeable happens to you; keep your emotions in check.
● Exercise patience with the light of reason combined with faith in God.
● Practice patience in a workman-like fashion, as part of your daily routine.
● Recognize that all things that happen to us, financial, spiritual, career, or otherwise, are foreseen and allowed by God.
● Ask yourself, "What can I learn from this experience, Lord?" when confronted with your own impatience.
● Success does not happen overnight.
● A handful of patience is worth more than a bushel of brains.
● Display compassion for others involved in issues that require your patience.
● Remember to be positive while practicing patience.

[The Biblical Perspective] *Patience*

And said, Naked came I out of my mother's womb, and naked shall I return thither: the
LORD gave, and the LORD hath taken away; blessed be the name of the LORD.
Job 1:21

The story of Job is one of perseverance through patience. Job was given leprosy and he lost his family, money, and worldly possessions as a test of faith. This seems to be a sad story, but we know that God used it to teach Job, and us, a lesson. First, we must always remember that family, health, wealth, and other good fortune are merely blessings on loan from God. We are blessed to have them and should care for them accordingly.

Throughout our lives, we may be faced with many situations that seem untenable: an abusive boss, a family conflict, unpleasant financial circumstances, and so on. These situations may not be the equivalent of leprosy, but they sure consume our time and money, and they can make life seem miserable.

However, when compared to the trials and tribulations of Job, our daily challenges are minute. In addition, we are usually responsible for our own unhappiness. However, thankfully, we can always take positive action and correct our course.

In the Book of Job, Job finally said, "Hey God, how about a little something for the effort?" God responded, "Don't question my authority, but you're right. I have been a little harsh on you." Job then had all his riches returned ten-fold. Patience is a grace that is as difficult to exhibit. Patience is necessary and it is as hard to come by. It is precious when it is possessed.

Guest Commentary

On Patience
by Gene Ward, PhD

Patience is not a natural virtue for most people, including myself. Some cultures stress it more than others, but overall it's an individual's take on the world and how we use the 86,400 seconds per day we are allotted, or the 2.2 billion seconds we have in a lifetime to waste or worry about. Patience is how we handle people we can't stand, or situations we want to get out of. Our impatience seeks a way of escape, often irrationally, which usually ends up with negative consequences.

Because of this, patience has never been my strong suit; it has been something I've had to learn through the school of hard knocks. Too often impatience was a function of my self-centeredness, living life on my terms, my time schedule, and my feelings. I didn't show concern for the constraints or considerations of others. I played a lot of football and as the quarterback and co-captain I was taught to take advantage of the weaknesses of my opponents. Later, as a businessman, I had to outsmart and out-maneuver the competition. Now as an elected official, I'm supposed to take advantage of every moment to promote myself for re-election.

However, now I'm a believer and I see patience as something entirely different. It's as if I've changed clocks and time zones. Now I'm on God's timing, instead of mine. In the past I mistakenly went after seizing days that I wasn't supposed to. As a believer, I have come to realize that not every day is for me to seize. I have also learned that planning and goal setting, if channeled through the Lord, curb impatience as a default reaction. I have my plan, but it is the Lord who will help implement it, or it's not what I want.

Everything has its own time. Leaders are known for their vision of the future, or ability to see things that others can't. People who consider eternity can be more patient than those who think only in terms of the here and now. Patience doesn't come naturally, it comes spiritually! Thankfully, God is patient with us as He teaches us patience and dependence upon His perfect timing.

Patience is an extraordinarily important,
yet underrated principle for success.
Patience is a virtue.
Patience doesn't come naturally.

[Principle Seven]
Attitude

My son, forget not my law; but let thine heart keep my commandments: For length of days, and long life, and peace, shall they add to thee. Let not mercy and truth forsake thee: bind them about thy neck; write them upon the table of thine heart: So shalt thou find favour and good understanding in the sight of God and man.

Proverbs 3:1-4

During my brief career in politics, I developed a self-centered attitude and my priorities were askew. I was filled with hubris and self-importance. After losing my race for Congress, I was out of work for a year. It was an extraordinarily humbling experience. I could not understand why I could not get hired by any local company. It seemed I was in the middle of an unbelievably bad run of luck. In retrospect, I can see now that the Lord had determined that it was time for me to get a taste of humble pie. And boy, did I need it!

I reflected on my religious beliefs and all the blessings God had showered me with during my life. I was healthy, had a loving family, and had an unlimited future. I had hope! I began to realize that the Lord has great things planned for all of us. Each day we can decide how we are going to feel emotionally. With Christ, we have hope, and with hope we can make it through any adversity.

The way you look at things programs your life. If you feel it, see it, believe it, it will be so, if it is in accordance with God's will. Therefore it is vital that we have a positive outlook on life. As many have said, what you think is what you will become. You have the power to determine how you will feel. You can decide how you are going to treat and interact with others. The more positively you treat other people, the better you will be treated. Smile at others, and they smile right back.

The business world recognizes the importance of having a positive attitude. At J.D. Edwards, they "believe that a person's success is due eight-five percent to attitude and fifteen percent to ability. Nothing reflects a good attitude more than the willingness to work hard. J.D. Edwards asks that every employee provide a solid, honest day's work-every day."[8]

After a tough year, I got my act together and refocused my priorities. It caused me to reflect on the blessings that really mattered. I decided to change my attitude to one of gratitude and concern for others. Things like getting my name in the paper were no longer important to me. My family took center stage again. I paid more attention to my loving wife's desires than my own. Her faith in me never faltered. My children learned valuable lessons by watching me go through this experience. They were used to seeing Dad on TV and now Dad was unable to get back on track. I became grateful for the simple things in life and this made me a better person. I began to look at the bright side of life and I never gave up hope. Each new day brought new opportunities and possibilities.

Consider This:

● *Who then is a faithful and wise servant, whom his lord hath made ruler over his household, to give them meat in due season? Blessed is that servant, whom his lord when he cometh shall find so doing.*

Matthew 24:45-46

[8]http://www.jdealumni.org/culturedocument?PHPSESSID=d94aaf4c31dd09f97e08608059fde639

● *Things turn out best for people who make the best of the way things turn out.*
  John Wooden

● *Take a moment to thank God for your friends, family, health, and other blessings that you may take for granted every day.*

During World War II, the United States Marines were asked to conduct an amphibious landing on Iwo Jima-an island that was essentially hardened lava that offered no cover or concealment. The enemy had months and months to prepare reinforced defensive positions dug into the hardened lava and they prepared defensive and interlocking zones of fire to cut down advancing troops. Given these facts, the Marines could have held a negative, defeatist attitude and offered a million excuses to higher command why this was an untenable mission. Instead, they said they could do it, and they did.

If they were able to overcome such odds, then you can overcome the problems that you are facing too. Stay positive. When you are tackling projects in the workplace or at home, approach them with an open mind and an uplifting attitude. Ask yourself how you can make the project successful while accomplishing the mission at hand.

During the depths of the 1982 recession, President Ronald Reagan told the nation that we were on our way back-that things were going to get better. He did this nearly every day. Despite negative trade numbers and an increasing national deficit and inflation figures, Reagan remained positive. Eventually the country became bullish on America again, and our country turned around. Reagan even ran a famous ad campaign about this issue called, "Morning in America." People believed it was a new day. Reagan's positive attitude was contagious. America caught Reagan fever and the country came back in a big way-all because of one man's positive attitude.

What you focus on becomes your reality. Seek positive outcomes and that is what you will end up with. Seek and you shall receive. Seek the positive. Focus on Christ. Seek the Lord, and you will receive his blessings.

Consider This:

● *And all things, whatsoever ye shall ask in prayer, believing, ye shall receive.*
  Matthew 21:22

● *Whether you think you can or you can't, you're probably right.*
  Henry Ford

● *When faced with a daunting challenge, do you "look at the bright side" of the issue, or are you a complainer?*

You have a choice to make. You can go through life with a scowl on your face and a poor attitude or you can look at life as a blessing, going through each day with a positive attitude. You will be surprised at how many things start "to go your way," almost miraculously with the proper attitude.

*And this is the confidence that we have in Him, that, if we ask any thing according to
His will, He heareth us: And if we know that He hear us, whatsoever we ask,
we know that we have the petitions that we desired of him.*
1 John 5:14-15

When I was a young Marine going to night school to get my college degree, my friends made fun of me. They ridiculed my efforts and said I would never make it. When they teased me, I brushed it off and stayed on track. I stayed positive, focused on my degree and finally got it. I asked for the Lord's help and took positive action. I focused and received in accordance with God's will. Despite what looked like an incredibly long journey I stayed positive.

It is often that way in life. When you try to achieve something of merit, people will put you down. Not for any particular reason, but just because as human beings we are flawed. We have fallen from grace and have to work at seeing the positive side of things. It is easy to be negative, but is also an empty destination.

A few years later, when I ran for a seat in the state legislature, people made fun of me. They told me I had no chance. After all, what made me think I was so special? When I was trying to raise funds for my campaign, one man sent me a million dollars-in monopoly money. I stayed focused on the goal and remained positive. I never dwelt on the negative and I knew I was going to win. I believed it. I saw it. I prayed for it. I felt God's hand guiding me and on my second attempt, I won!

My wife and I have a big family and spend a lot of money on food. On one occasion, we hadn't stocked up in a while and I wondered how we were going to make it to the next payday. Then I remembered that the Lord always provides. I chose to trust Him, knowing that the Lord would provide. When I got home, there was a check for $1,300 from an unexpected source in my mailbox.

While still recovering from my loss in the congressional race, I was teaching classes part-time and also working as a security guard. However, I was not back on track professionally. Our income was much lower than what it had been in the previous year due to my selfish decision to seek a congressional seat. One day our landlord drove by and saw that there was termite damage to our home. Upon further inspection, he deemed the dwelling unsafe and gave us forty-five days to vacate. I dreaded this for several reasons. First, it was the Christmas season. We were struggling financially and having a hard time paying the rent. My credit was terrible because I had declared bankruptcy two years earlier. I needed to find a place to live for my family, which included my wife's parents, who also lived with us. I had no money, no credit, and little time, but I had the Lord. I focused on the challenge and prayed for the Lord's help. Failure was not an option.

The next day, I bumped into Dave Carlson, a friend of mine at the gas station. The housing market was just starting to heat up and Dave was an expert. As a retired army officer and real estate agent, he made some wise investments and was really into helping others. I told Dave of my situation and asked him he if could help us find a home. He said he would come by our house that very afternoon. I was thrilled to have his guidance. There is no doubt in my mind that he was sent by the Lord.

We searched the internet together and found some homes we could afford, based on my income. As Dave and I narrowed our search, we found a unit that fit our needs. It was empty and we could move in within thirty days. It was a forty year-old home that needed some work. It was in a depressed section of town, with the normal problems associated with that sort of area, but it was big, clean, and had a huge yard by Hawaii standards. My wife and I decided it was the right place.

We made the offer through Dave, who suggested that we offer $10,000 over the seller's asking price to ensure that we got the house. I agreed because time was of the essence for us-we had to get a new home and the clock was running. Dave called me back and said the seller was a little nervous about our credit and that our financing might fall through. The seller wanted a non-refundable check for $1,000 as earnest money. My heart sank. I told Dave things were really tight for us financially and that I did not have that kind of money. After a moment's thought, Dave said that he would loan us the $1,000.

As I was working with Dave, I was also working with a mortgage broker. I told the broker that I didn't care what interest rate I had to pay. I just wanted financing. Due to my poor credit, there were a lot of hurdles, however the mortgage broker was a positive guy with a "can do" attitude. With his help and hard work, I ended up getting approved for financing. It was for 100 percent of the purchase price plus the closing costs. It was another miracle.

We closed on the house and moved in on New Year's day, 2004. Upon closing we received $5,000 to help with appliance upgrades because Dave wrote that into the loan and sale documents. Dave later told me that I could keep the $1,000 dollar and spend it on the house and my large family.

I don't know what would have happened without Dave's help, generosity, and positive belief that we could get the deal done. To Dave, everything was possible and there were no limits when it came to helping others achieve their dream of home ownership. Clearly, the Lord stepped in and touched Dave's heart and allowed us to buy a home. We remained positive though the whole ordeal. We prayed daily on this issue. As you can imagine, the holidays are a stressful time; add the immediate need for housing and the holiday joy evaporates. My wife and I never lost faith in God and knew that when our attitudes were Christ-filled and positive, we would succeed. And we did.

We bought the house for $249,000. I recently had it appraised and it came in at $460,000, before any major renovations were made. The Lord blessed us with an additional $200,000 in equity just by being in that house. Today we remain as grateful as ever about our home. We'll always have a special place in our heart for Dave.

Like the bird in the tree, we never have to wonder where our next meal is going to come from. The Lord God will always take care of us.

But my God shall supply all your need according to his riches in glory by Christ Jesus.
Philippians 4:19

The way you look at life determines what you see. Look at life in a positive Christian fashion, and you will live a positive life. If you are in need, as the verse above says, then surely God will answer you, provided it is His will. Contemplative prayer and a positive attitude will get you what you need.

Consider This:

● *Happiness is an attitude. We either make ourselves miserable, or happy and strong. The amount of work is the same.*

Francesca Reigler

● *Birds never fret about where their next meal is going to come from. Do you believe that God will always provide and be there for you?*

Application:

● Start each day with a prayer of thanks.
● Ask for God's guidance during the day.
● Ask God to give you the ability to help others.
● Dispatch negative thoughts immediately.
● Refuse to dwell on the slights that may come your way.
● Having a positive attitude is contagious.
● Share the benefits of a positive outlook with others.
● Refuse to engage in gossip.
● Your thoughts are reflections of your soul.
● Every action starts with a thought.
● Eliminate fear, for if God is with you, and He is, then who can be against you!
● Act with positive and decisive action when confronted with evil of any sort.
● Do not dwell on the evil, but focus on the positive through positive action.
● Volunteer to help others as a way of recharging your attitude.
● Display a "can do" attitude in all professional undertakings.
● Make positive thoughts habitual.
● Have high hopes!
● Be positive!

[The Biblical Perspective] *Attitude*

*And he heard the words of Laban's sons, saying, Jacob hath taken away all that was
our father's; and of that which was our father's hath he gotten all this glory.
And Jacob beheld the countenance of Laban, and, behold, it was not toward him
as before. And the LORD said unto Jacob, Return unto the land of thy fathers,
and to thy kindred; and I will be with thee. And Jacob sent and called Rachel and Leah
to the field unto his flock, And said unto them, I see your father's countenance, that it
is not toward me as before; but the God of my father hath been with me. And ye know
that with all my power I have served your father. And your father hath deceived me,
and changed my wages ten times; but God suffered him not to hurt me.*

Genesis 31:1-7

The verses above are a good example of how someone's attitude can have
an effect on an individual. In this case, Laban and his sons had a bad attitude
toward Jacob. That caused Jacob great frustration because he had done all of
the right things and had treated his father-in-law Laban well. He worked
hard for Laban. Yet, Laban displayed an ungrateful attitude toward Jacob and
cheated him out of a portion of his wages.

Jacob was wise enough to know-with some help from God-that you
cannot change how other people think. You can only control how you react to
them. It makes no sense to strike back or engage in "tit for tat." Just move on.
That's what Jacob did. His conscience was clear because he didn't do
anything wrong. He knew that despite their ill feelings toward him, once he
left, their feelings would be of no consequence.

Have you ever worked with someone who was so negative that you
wanted to quit your job rather than continue working at that company?
Believe it or not, this is all too common in our world. A negative attitude can
poison a family, a workplace, even a nation. However, a positive attitude can

be just as powerful and produce blessings for all involved.

Entire books have been written about the power of a positive attitude. In order to be successful, be the opposite of Laban and his sons. Show a positive attitude to all-especially those who help you. You must do this in order to be successful. A positive attitude can't enable you to be good at everything, but a positive attitude will make you better at everything than a negative attitude will!

Guest Commentary

Riki Ellison
Three-time Super Bowl Champion
and Successful Business Executive
Interview about Attitude on February 15, 2008

Riki, you have been a winner all your life; at USC, the 49ers, and now as the president and founder of Missile Defense Advocacy Alliance. Were you a "born winner?"

Bob, I was blessed to be surrounded by winners and people with a positive attitude-since as early as I can remember. The people who had an influence on my life when I was growing up were just amazing. They infused a deep and strong moral compass and value structure in my soul.

My Uncle Riki - my namesake-was a Mori Chief; a man of integrity, from Christ Church New Zealand. He had a farm. I spent a lot of time with him. He taught me leadership, heart, and morals-to be humble and generous. He had a profound influence on my life. He left a lasting impression and he was an example of how to be a man that I still carry on today.

My mother and I left New Zealand in 1968 and we moved to a ranch in Arizona. Our closest neighbors where two miles away. It was wide open country. The ranch foreman befriended me in a grandfatherly way. He was Americano personified, a World War II tank commander under General George Patton, the embodiment of old fashioned American values. He taught me about football and life. It is on the Arizona ranch that I saw my first football game on a black and white TV. Right then and there I decided to become a USC football player. That's when I began to dream big dreams. Open country, fresh air-there were no limits to my dreaming. The next thing I knew, I got a college scholarship.

In football, college and the pros, who influenced you as a mentor?

My USC College football coach was the great John Robinson. He was a player's coach and made the game fun. He boiled the game down to its most basic and raw essence-speed and power; man-on-man. You had to measure up and compete. USC was loaded with talent and you had to demonstrate one-on-one that you had what it took.

In the pros the 49ers Coach Bill Walsh was a true mentor. He took the game to the next level. He transcended the brawn vs. brawn to add a new dimension to your game. He focused on positive attitude, preparation, practice, being quicker to the play, and thinking-always thinking. He really refined the game into an art form.

You have been injured several times. Some of these injuries would have ended athletic careers. Were you ever worried? Did your injuries affect you mentally?

My core beliefs were so strong that injuries never affected me. A few knee surgeries were merely bumps in the road. I would not let them get in the way of my dreams formulated when I was twelve years old, on that Arizona ranch. I set goals for myself; I dreamed that I would play for USC, that I would marry a USC cheerleader, that we'd beat Notre Dame, and we'd win the Rose Bowl and a national championship. I did all of those things. I would not let injuries or distractions sidetrack me from my goals. I was driven and always had a positive attitude.

Were there ever times when you saw your team was behind in points and the chances seemed bleak, but you knew you were going to win, because you had the attitude of a winner?

Absolutely. Winning is an attitude, a belief, a special feeling that you can overcome any obstacle. A winning attitude has to come from inside. You can see it in your teammates' eyes. Most of the time, we had already won the game before we stepped on the field against the teams I played in college and in the pros This winning attitude is special, but it only takes one or two negative guys to break the chain.

You were a successful in college and the pros. You then left the game. How was the transition, and how did it affect your attitude.

Tough transition. One minute you go from being the best in your profession, and then you're not. You are out. A lot of guys try to stay around the game, because there is a comfort level. When you go out into the real world, you have to start all over. You are back at square one in a field or profession, where you may not know very much and are competing against others who have been in the field for quite some time.

Yeah, the transition was tough. I think I read somewhere that seventy-eight percent of former pro-football players end up divorced or in bankruptcy. I got divorced. The transition was difficult. It was a big adjustment. It hits the egos of many guys. I went through it, but I knew that if I kept fighting, striving, and competing, I would succeed-- and I did. MDAA is the defacto leader nationally in supporting missile defense, protecting American citizens.

One last thing-how has your faith in God played a role in your life?

Faith is my pillar. It is where I get my blessings; I have been blessed with talent and drive. I did not understand this until I had to start over. I rediscovered my faith after I left football. My faith kept me going. It is a daily part of my life, a constant. I pray, read the Bible, and I try to touch other people in a positive way.

You have a choice to make.
You can go through life with a scowl
and a poor attitude or – you can look at life
as a blessing, going through each day
with a positive attitude. You will
be surprised at how many things
will start to "go your way," almost
miraculously with the proper attitude.

[Principle Eight]
Fidelity

And foundest his heart faithful before thee, and madest a covenant with him to give the land

of the Canaanites, the Hittites, the Amorites, and the Perizzites, and the Jebusites, and the

Girgashites, to give it, I say, to his seed, and hast performed thy words; for thou art righteous.

Nehemiah 9:8

In today's world it is easy to be tempted to drift off course. In fact, Focus on the Family says that more than one-third of all men admit to having at least one extramarital tryst.[9] I have seen men who have strayed and it cost them dearly. One let his libido drive him off course and another let his lack of financial fidelity destroy the multi-million dollar business he built.

The first man was an old Marine Corps buddy of mine. The Marine Corps motto is "Semper Fidelis" which means "Always Faithful." Clearly, this is an organization that has lived up to its motto. The basic training for both officers and enlisted men teaches integrity and being true to the wholesome values of the Marines. Most Marines carry these lessons with them for life, as evidenced by the old saying, "Once a Marine, always a Marine." My old Marine friend and I were both fully indoctrinated with the same values, especially, fidelity.

We met as young Marines in Hawaii when we were in the Corps together the early 1980s. However, even back then he did not seem like a trustworthy

[9]http://www.family.org/lifechallenges/A000000236.cfm

fellow. In fact, mutual friends nicknamed him "diode," which is an electrical component that only lets current flow one way, because he was totally self-absorbed. Eventually we lost touch, moved on, and went our separate ways.

I bumped into him three years later. He was selling cars and invited me and my buddy to his house for a beer. I went and enjoyed talking about old times. However, it wasn't all fun and games because his lovely young bride had just gone through a miscarriage and was an emotional basket case. He was attentive to her needs and showed an admirable and loving side. We finished our beers and promised to stay in touch. We didn't and I lost track of him.

Ten years later, while running for office, I bumped into him again. He was an automobile sales manager and was doing well financially. We had a lot in common at that point-we had kids about the same age, lived in the same community, and shared similar political views. He even donated to my campaign. We stayed in touch casually, seeing each other as neighbors do at the store, community events, etc. However, we didn't do anything socially because our schedules were hectic.

Several years later, while attending a football game, I saw him in the stands, but he wasn't sitting with his wife. He told me that he was on the tail end of a divorce and we could talk about it later. I was shocked. He had been married for twenty years. What would cause him to seek a divorce?

We had lunch that week and he told me that he "just didn't want to live with her anymore." That was it. I asked him a few more questions thinking that something must have happened. Nope. No affairs, no financial problems, nothing. He just wanted to find someone else. As best I could tell, he just wanted to feed natural desires he had for other women. As our conversation continued and he told me about his recent sexual escapades. He was a handsome man, made a good living, and he was in great shape. He told me that there are many women in his age bracket looking for a relationship. It was a target rich environment-meaning he was sleeping with a lot of women.

After I left my lunch with him, the enormity of what he had done with his life began to sink in. I thought he was extraordinarily selfish. He destroyed his family because he wanted to be with other women. The devastation that he inflicted upon his wife, children, and extended family can not be overstated. He blew his family apart. Needless to say, his wife was crushed. She did not want a divorce. She thought everything was just fine. She had given him the best twenty years of her life, bore three children, and a miscarriage of twins. Her life revolved around the family, and his actions changed all of that.

He still does not fully understand what he has done. When I asked him if her family was angry at him, he said they shouldn't be because he always treated them well. What makes this story so disturbing is that this wasn't some momentary lapse of judgment or an unplanned indiscretion. No, this was a calculated move that he carried out methodically. But we serve a big God-one who answers prayer, so I often pray that my old Marine buddy will come to his senses and return to his family.

If you are looking for a key to success in your business and personal life, then look no further than Christian fidelity, which includes being faithful to God, yourself, family, friends, and your business associates. Christian fidelity is a testament to God's fidelity to us as His creations. His love for us has endured despite the unfaithfulness of His chosen people. So much so, that He sent His only begotten son into the world to save all of humankind.

The fruit of promises kept, confidence, and trust, is love and mutual respect that blossoms in all phases of life-personal and business. A man who can remain faithful will be trusted and lifted up by the Lord.

Consider This:

● *Hear my prayer, O LORD, give ear to my supplications: in thy faithfulness answer me, and in thy righteousness.*

Psalm 143:1

● *There are two kinds of fidelity-that of dogs and that of cats; and you gentlemen, have the fidelity of cats who never leave the house.*

Napoleon Bonaparte

● *Do you realize that fidelity in marriage elevates sexual activity from merely a physical experience to one that is an expression of love and unity?*

The second story is about fidelity as it relates to business relationships and agreements. "Steve" had three successful companies and was a leader in the business community. He was a member of the Chamber of Commerce, on the boards of various community organizations. He was a "mover and shaker."

What no one knew was that Steve was living on borrowed time. Steve was the majority and controlling partner of the "Hawaii XYZ Company" and had a minority partner that lived several thousands of miles away. Steve charged all the business expenses from his other related companies to the Hawaii XYZ Company: personnel, his car, office, phone, travel, donations-everything. For years, Steve's silent minority partner sat by and trusted Steve, unaware that he was being ripped off.

Steve's business partner became curious as to why he never made any money while Steve seemed to be doing so well. Finally, after several years of acrimony, the minority partner sued Steve in court for tens of thousands of dollars of lost profits and damages. Steve and his attorney settled out of court. Because he was in gross violation of any standard business practices, Steve was forced to liquidate his three companies and finally pay his partner his due.

Steve was publicly embarrassed when the news was printed in the local newspapers. His professional and personal life and reputation were in a complete shambles. His dishonesty and lack of fidelity to his business partner caused his downfall and he paid a heavy price.

Today, he is a changed man, surrounded by worry and angst. His days of riding high are just a distant memory. I regret that he had to go through his ordeal. I take no joy in watching others struggle. I do hope he has learned the importance of fidelity.

Consider This:

● *Fidelity is seven-tenths of business success.*

  James Parton

● *Are you ever been tempted to take advantage of a situation like the one Steve was in? If so, what are you doing to protect yourself from falling into this trap?*

Our Vietnam POWs are a great example of what fidelity is supposed to look like. I have gotten to know some of these men personally. They are quite an extraordinary bunch of men. During their time as prisoners, they were tortured for information, subjected to propaganda and brain washing. They revealed little or nothing. I remember one POW telling me that when he was being tortured by the Vietnamese for the names of all the pilots in his squadron, he gave them the names of the guys on his high school football team.

One of these POWs, Jerry Coffee-spent seven years in captivity and told his remarkable story in a book entitled, **Beyond Survival.** He wrote about having faith in our country, family, comrades, and in God. A few prisoners collaborated with the enemy, but guys like Coffee were the norm. They were loyal to our country.

In his book, Coffee said that the goal of the Vietnam POWs was to "return with honor" and their motto was "unity over self." The experience made Coffee love his country even more once he returned home. He never lost faith in God. Instead, faith is what got him through his ordeal and in turn allowed him to remain faithful to his country. He has turned the lost years in a POW cell into a public-speaking career. He shares the POW experience with audiences across the nation and he tells people about the importance of hope, faith, and fidelity to God and country.

The story of Vietnam POW Jim Stockdale is truly amazing. When Stockdale learned that the Vietnamese were going to use him for a public relations photo opportunity, he cut his scalp with his a sharp object so his hair and face were covered with blood. Upon their return to his holding room, the Vietnamese were angry and the guards were ordered to clean Jim up-they still intended to use him for the photo. After he was cleaned up, they left him alone in his holding room. When the Vietnamese returned again, Stockdale's face was a bloody mess. He had taken the stool he was sitting on and beat himself to a bloody pulp. The Vietnamese were not going to be able to use Stockdale for their PR purposes. Jim Stockdale was faithful to his country.

Stockdale's actions were heroic. He loved America and was not about to let the Vietnamese use him to further their cause. When he returned home, he was awarded the Congressional Medal of Honor.

Consider This:

● *I beheld the transgressors, and was grieved; because they kept not thy word.*
Psalms 119:158

● *To God, thy countrie, and they friend be true.*
Bill Vaughan

● *Do you have the same type of fidelity as James Stockdale that will help you remain loyal despite tough circumstances and difficult people?*

I have one more story to share about fidelity. This time it relates to a personal friendship I had when I was a state legislator some years ago. I got to know and confide in a lobbyist whom I will call Rex. I met with Rex often. He was a nice man-ingratiating, friendly, and supportive. I could always count on Rex for donations and other considerations in substantial amounts for my reelection to the State House.

My natural political views happened to coincide with the interests he represented so we worked together to advance common interests. I had many chats and discussions with Rex and I felt like we were really developing a solid relationship. We became good friends, or so I thought.

Occasionally, I would see Rex in the Capitol hallways and he would always say "Hi" or greet me in a friendly fashion, but his demeanor was much more reserved and subdued than in private. I attributed this to the fact that he did not want to be seen as being too chummy with a member of my party affiliation.

However, when we had meetings which consisted of only party members, Rex still treated me differently. He never let on that he was friendly with me; he kept me at arms length. I found this strange and disturbing. Later I asked him about this behavior and he just laughed it off. I felt duped. I thought this guy was a genuine friend, but he wasn't. He was a very good lobbyist and as such, made me feel like I was special, like I was his friend. Boy, was I naive.

After I left elective office, I wanted to stay in touch with him. We had lunch or coffee a few times-always at my initiative, but the longer I was out of office, the less responsive he became to e-mails or phone messages.

I saw him recently at a community event. He made a joke about my political views and walked away. It bothered me for several days. Coincidentally, I saw him a few days later at the Pacific Club during lunch. He walked by me, shook my and hand, and said, "How are you?" He clearly had forgotten my name. When I got home I talked to my wife about it. She said she always knew that Rex was a phony. She told me she could see right through him and his motives. Ah well, a lesson learned.

Consider This:

● *Nothing is more noble, nothing more venerable than fidelity. Faithfulness and truth are the most sacred excellences and endowments of the human mind.*

  Marcus Tullius Cicero

● *Can you recognize those who are not genuine, truthful, when they are hurling flattery your way? Beware, for they lack the fidelity of a true friend.*

Application:

● Be faithful to Jesus Christ our Lord.
● Be faithful to your spouse and family members.
● Be true in your business dealings.
● Be authentic in your interpersonal relations.
● Be a steward of your soul.
● Keep your commitments.
● Keep your promises.
● Be true to your country.

[The Biblical Perspective] *Fidelity*

Who then is a faithful and wise servant, whom his lord hath made ruler over his household, to give them meat in due season? Blessed is that servant, whom his lord when he cometh shall find so doing. Verily I say unto you, That he shall make him ruler over all his goods. But and if that evil servant shall say in his heart, My lord delayeth his coming; And shall begin to smite his fellow servants, and to eat and drink with the drunken; The lord of that servant shall come in a day when he looketh not for him, and in an hour that he is not aware of, And shall cut him asunder, and appoint him his portion with the hypocrites: there shall be weeping and gnashing of teeth.

  Matthew 24:45-51

We will be judged on how we care for the resources and or gifts that are placed in our care. There may be times that we are tested in this situation. We must exercise loyalty to a fault, knowing that we have an awesome responsibility to our God. We are blessed to be stewards of gifts, our relationships, and possessions, and we are ultimately responsible for how we act.

Clearly, we are expected and directed to be faithful to our Lord, our subordinates, our trustees-anyone who trusts us with responsibility. We are called to act with fidelity. We must be vigilant, ready, and act with the best interests of our charges.

The verses above suggest that we may be called to account at any time by the Lord, so we must be ready. Pain and heartache will be the result for those who do not act properly or exercise good stewardship over the gifts they are given to manage. We must be true and faithful.

Guest Commentary

On Fidelity

by John R. Bates
Colonel, United States Marine Corps (Ret.)

Anyone who has ever worn the Eagle, Globe, and Anchor of the United States Marine Corps does so with unwavering commitment to God, country, and Corps, in that order. As the saying goes: "Once a Marine, always a Marine." That is not just a slogan. It is a way of life and a heritage that must be honored until one's dying breath.

As commissioned officers, we seal our commitment with the oath of office:

"I, (state your full name) do solemnly swear (or affirm) that I will support and defend the Constitution of the United States against all enemies, both foreign or domestic, that I will bear true faith and allegiance to the same; that I take this obligation freely, without any mental reservation or purpose of evasion; and that I will well and faithfully discharge the duties of the office upon which I am about to enter; So help me God."

The enlisted oath is very similar with only minor changes. Ponder that oath for a moment. We are stating in public that with God's help, we will faithfully defend our country. Fidelity is by definition, faithfulness.

On December 17, 1966, I was assigned to Golf Company, Second Battalion, Fifth Marines, First Marine Division. We were headquartered in An Hoa, Vietnam. The land was beautifully green. The monsoons had begun and it was very hot, especially from mid-day until dark. We set out that morning on patrol seeking to engage the North Vietnamese Army and the Viet Cong a few miles north of An Hoa, near a village called Phu Loc 6.

After passing through Phu Loc 6 village, we encountered sniper fire. Fortunately, no Marines were killed or wounded in that initial engagement.

We spread our frontage and pushed the NVA back to the Song Thu Bon River where they sought a better position on an egg-shaped island, bounded in front by an open stretch of sand with the river to their rear.

Our platoon commander, William L. Buchanan, had us take firing positions at the edge of the vegetation while he called in an air strike. The Marine air violently tore the island to shreds and we assumed that we would soon be doing nothing more than taking a body count and collecting war souvenirs. What we didn't know is that the enemy had retreated into a complex cave network as the air strike began. Once lifted, the enemy surfaced and hit us hard as we were approaching the position.

Combat is always chaotic. This was to be no exception. Once in the open, our enemy fully engaged us with every weapon they owned. Moments later my body was slammed by an enemy round. I lay in the sand bleeding from an entrance wound through my right chest and an exit wound out my back. It was known to us from our combat life-saving classes as the proverbial "sucking chest wound." Few people are known to live after receiving such a wound.

It was all too apparent to me that my future was questionable. I lay there praying to God to allow me to live to fight another fight. From such an unusual observation point, I witnessed "fidelity" in what I believe to be its purest form. Lt. Buchanan covered me with his body while yelling into two different radio handsets. On one, he called for more air strikes to suppress the enemy. On the other, he calmly and methodically went through the nine-line brief to bring in an emergency medevac helicopter to get me to the field hospital. Lt. Buchanan loved his Marines and valued their lives as much or more than his own. He knowingly risked his own life for mine.

Through fading eyes, I saw both courage and fidelity. To those that have not had a similar experience, it is difficult to describe what a dramatic and inspirational moment that was. Lt. Buchanan was faithful to his charges. He showed me in the most personal of ways, just what "fidelity" truly meant.

If you are looking for a key to success
in your business and personal life,
then look no further than Christian fidelity,
which includes being faithful to God,
yourself, family, friends, and
your business associates.

[Principle Nine]
Goals

Suppose one of you wants to build a tower. Will he not first sit down and estimate the cost
to see if he has enough money to complete it? For if he lays the foundation and is not
able to finish it, everyone who sees it will ridicule him, saying, 'This fellow began to
build and was not able to finish.' Or suppose a king is about to go to war against
another king. Will he not first sit down and consider whether he is able with
ten thousand men to oppose the one coming against him with twenty thousand?
Luke 14:28-31

This might surprise you, but according to the Indiana Department of Education, *"Only about three percent of Americans have clearly written and defined goals. The other ninety-eight percent neglect to set goals, perhaps because they are afraid that they will not attain them."*[10]

The first part of this chapter will sound a little repetitive, however, it is the best example I can give of how I used goals firsthand-unknowingly-during the first forty years of my life. Goals give purpose to living. I have had clear, concise, and achievable goals throughout my adult life. This has always kept me busy, moving forward, and on track. I took small bites at success, one easy piece at a time. This enabled me to tackle each new challenge or goal with confidence knowing I could succeed. I think the story bears repeating.

After I graduated from high school, I joined the Marines. I went to boot

---

[10]http://www.doe.in.gov/octe/bme/newsletters/vocbusmay06.pdf

camp and was forcibly immersed and pushed into accomplishing my goal. The drill instructors did not give me much choice in the matter. They molded me and formed me into a Marine. Failure was not an option.

During my enlistment, I decided to get a college degree. I set a goal of my goal following my honorable discharge from the Marines.

In my personal life, I wanted to marry a beautiful local Polynesian woman who would be a good mother. I prayed big powerful prayers and was specific in dreaming of a dark-skinned girl with long flowing black hair and a nice shape. It took a couple of years and then God delivered a Polynesian angel into my life-my Samoan princess, Utufa'asili. She is exactly what I prayed for.

During my senior year in college I was a civilian preparing for life after college. With a wife and one child, I decided I needed to go back into the Marines and become an officer. This was a much harder goal because my motivation was not proper at the time. I was more concerned about what the Corps could do and provide for my young family, than about focusing on my ability to lead young Marines. It was a struggle, but I made it, just barely.

After my service in the Corps I wanted to get into business in Hawaii with a large company. I literally went door to door to hand out my resume in the industrial areas of Oahu. The day I was released from active duty, I was offered a job with C. Brewer. While at C. Brewer, I wanted to get ahead and be successful. The career path in the company did not appear favorable with my talents, so I went back to school to get an MBA to help me get ahead. After two years, more student loans and expenses, I secured my MBA.

Then my focus turned to politics. I was very concerned that Hawaii was going to legalize same-sex marriage. So I took action and ran for the State Legislature in 1994 against a pro-gay marriage legislator. I lost, but I was not discouraged because this was my first try.

In 1996, I focused on the goal of getting elected. It was an all-consuming passion for me. I started a television show on the public access channels (when there were only 22 channels) in order to increase my presence in the community. It worked well. Support showed up miraculously and money flowed in. Due to my focus on running, I was terminated from a job that I had taken a year earlier. However, I viewed the firing as a blessing as I could now campaign full-time. I was relentless in my quest and won a seat in the State Legislature in 1996.

In 2002, I decided to run for Congress. This was a rather lofty goal, but one I had long held to as an objective. As I mentioned earlier, I ran and lost. I drifted aimlessly for a year with my only goal being able to pay the bills, which was not much of a goal at all. I didn't have any direction. It was a terrible feeling. However, with Christ, I recovered and now I have lofty goals again. I know I can achieve great things with God's help. Using the tools that God has given me, I've discovered that there aren't any limitations.

Everyone who is successful has goals. There is an old saying, "If you don't know where you're going, any road will get you there." Without goals you will drift aimlessly like a boat in the water with no rudder and no direction. When you are young, it is easy to have goals because you believe everything is possible. You do not know that you "can't" do something. As you get older, your goals become much more modest and conservative because you do not want to risk losing "what you have."

Consider This:

● *Success is about having, excellence is about being. Success is about having money and fame, but excellence is being the best you can be.*

Mike Ditka

● *The future you see is the future you get.*

Robert G. Allen

Sports figures are great examples of goal setters and achievers. One of the main reasons is because their performance is so easy to measure with statistics. One of the most famous goal-driven athletes of our time is Michael Jordan. Clearly, he was the greatest basketball player to ever lace up a pair of sneakers. No one before or since has had the impact on the sport that he has. Surprisingly, Jordan was not a child prodigy like Kobe Bryant or Moses Malone. Instead, he became the greatest player of all time through hard work and goal setting, among other things.

This is what Michael said about goals: "I approach everything step by step ... I had always set short-term goals. As I look back, each one of the steps or successes led to the next one. When I got cut from the varsity team as a sophomore in high school, I learned something. I knew I never wanted to feel that bad again... So I set a goal of becoming a starter on the varsity. That's what I focused on all summer. When I worked on my game, that's what I thought about. When it happened, I set another goal, a reasonable, manageable goal that I could realistically achieve if I worked hard enough... I guess I approached it with the end in mind. I knew exactly where I wanted to go, and I focused on getting there. As I reached those goals, they built on one another. I gained a little confidence every time I came through... If [your goal is to become a doctor]... and you're getting Cs in biology then the first thing you have to do is get Bs in biology and then As. You have to perfect the first step and then move on to chemistry or physics."[11]

Take those small steps. Otherwise you open yourself up to all kinds of frustration. Where would your confidence come from if the only measure of success was becoming a doctor? If you tried as hard as you could and didn't become a doctor would that mean your life was a failure? Of course not. All those steps are like pieces of a puzzle. They come together to form a picture.

[11]*I Can't Accept Not Trying: Michael Jordan on the Pursuit of Excellence.* Published by HarperSanFrancisco, a division of HarperCollinsPublishers (ISBN 0-06-25119)

Not everyone is going to be the greatest, but you can still be a success. Step by step. I can't see any other way of accomplishing anything.

Consider This:

● *A wise man thinks ahead; a fool doesn't and even brags about it!*
  Proverbs 13:16

● *If you want to live a happy life, tie it to a goal, not to people or things.*
  Albert Einstein

● *Do you have goals that will improve the quality of your life and those around you? If so, what are they?*

Arnold Schwarzenegger is another example of a goal and purpose-driven individual. I have studied and admired Arnold for many years. He came to America with a well developed body and superior genetics and he eventually became a bodybuilding champion.

While at the height of his career, he saw bodybuilding as a door to acting. He wanted to be a star like Reg Park of the old Hercules movies; it seemed like a natural and logical transition to Arnold. Hollywood insiders laughed at him. His name, thick accent, and huge body all worked against him. Fifteen years after retiring from bodybuilding, he was the top box office draw in Hollywood.

Arnold could have had the pick of many, many beautiful women in Hollywood. But he decided to "marry well." He married Maria Shriver, American "royalty"- a Kennedy. I am certain he loves her, but I am also certain that being a Kennedy made Maria all that more attractive to Arnold.

I had heard speculation for several years that Arnold was going to run for governor of California. He had conquered the movie industry. Next he would conquer politics. He had a new goal and began to prepare himself. He laid his public policy groundwork with an after school ballot initiative to give himself political creditability. Through preparation, direction, and circumstance, Arnold was elected governor of California.

How did Arnold accomplish so much? Why was he able to achieve so much in comparison to more capable people? Listen to Arnold's answer: "Most of the people I observed couldn't make astonishing advances because they never had faith in themselves. They had a hazy picture of what they wanted to look like someday, but they doubted they could realize it. Ultimately they didn't put out the kind of effort I did because they didn't feel they had a chance to make it. And of course, starting with that premise, they didn't."

In the course of your goal setting, don't forget to include helping others. If you do that you will find many more people attracted to you through the invisible hand of God. If you love what you do, and provide a service or some sort of value to others, then you will be abundantly blessed.

Consider This:

● *Except the LORD build the house, they labour in vain that build it: except the LORD keep the city, the watchman waketh but in vain.*

Psalm 127:1

● *By prevailing over all obstacles and distractions, one may unfailingly arrive at his chosen goal or destination.*

Christopher Columbus

● *Set your goals high, and don't stop till you get there.*

Bo Jackson

● *Do you possess an unrelenting commitment toward your goals?*

One last thing about setting goals-you will reach your goals as long as they are in line with God's plan for your life. In an earlier chapter I stated, "If you want to make God laugh, make plans." That is true. If your goals are in line with God's plans for you, you will achieve them. If they are not, you will probably be setting yourself up for failure and heartache. Seek God in prayer when establishing your goals. God usually has three answers for all of our prayer requests: yes, no, or not now, I have something better planned for you. Let me amplify.

I loved basketball and always wanted to be a division one college basketball player. It was for the wrong reasons. I longed for the perfect woman and I thought athletics was the way to attract the right one. I thought that by playing college basketball, I would be popular and women would find me attractive. I tried out for the college team and was cut. I was devastated. God answered my prayer and desires in a different way. He had someone better for me in mind. Four months later, I met my wife. My short-term goal of being a hoop star was unnecessary to secure my long-term goal of a beautiful loving wife.

Ideas are not goals until you write them down. Once you write them down, they become real, otherwise they are just thoughts and daydreams. Pray about your goals and ask God if they match what he has planned for you. Be open to new ideas or short-term paths that may help you reach your long-term goal.

Application:

- Pray about your goals to ensure you are on the right path.
- Write your goals down, otherwise, they are merely thoughts of fancy.
- Ensure that all of your goals are in concert with other goals.
- Your goals must be measurable and attainable.
- State your goals in a positive manner, for example, instead of saying, "I will quit drinking," say, "I want to get healthy and rid my body of toxins."

- Address your goals with specificity. Don't say you want to send your children to a private school. Instead specify what private school you want to send your children to.
- Set lofty goals that require work and effort. When you shoot for the stars, you will always reach the sky.
- Share your goals carefully with those that will encourage and motivate you.
- Review your goals periodically.
- Take action daily toward meeting your goals.
- Possess an unrelenting passion for your goals.
- Drive and ambition are vital to your success.

[The Biblical Perspective] *Goals*

For if any be a hearer of the word, and not a doer, he is like unto a man beholding his natural face in a glass: For he beholdeth himself, and goeth his way, and straightway forgetteth what manner of man he was. But whoso looketh into the perfect law of liberty, and continueth therein, he being not a forgetful hearer, but a doer of the work, this man shall be blessed in his deed.

James 1:23-25

This passage from the book of James makes it abundantly clear that man has a responsibility to listen to the Word of God and be a doer of the Word. Upon hearing the Word, man should be infused with many things-among them is industry and initiative.

Have you ever considered your unique gifts and the source of these gifts? God gives us an overflowing abundance of blessings. These gifts and special abilities were not given to only meet our selfish needs. We have been blessed with God-given gifts for the betterment of others. Therefore we should be willing to use these blessings for the greater good. Otherwise, we are destined to have unfulfilled lives.

First, a man must recognize his unique God-given gifts. Then he must take the initiative to make a plan. You cannot sit idle under the shade tree of life. Sorrow comes to the man who sits idle, watching the world go by. Initiative is exercising your God-given ability to get out of your chair and do something. Undertake a great endeavor! Dream big dreams! Nothing is impossible with God.

When making your plans to use God's gifts, you need milestones, or goals. These will enable you to measure your progress toward fulfilling your dream. Goals are critical for achieving your grand plans. A man must have goals; if he does not, he is akin to a ship with no direction. If a man has no destination, he will go where the tide takes him.

God has given you a finite time on this earth. You have a responsibility to use His gifts. This may not mean climbing Mount Everest; it may be as challenging as raising your children well, in a hostile environment. But you must exercise your initiative and set goals in order to accomplish those things which God has ordained for you. Remember, faith without works is dead!

Guest Commentary

Goals and Initiative

by Patrick T. Brent
U.S. Marine Veteran, Entrepreneur, Philanthropist

We all have our heroes. My favorites are individuals who have triumphed over difficult and overwhelming odds. History is full of such heroes. In my opinion, Ray Kroc, the founder of McDonald's, was a hero.

At the age of fifty-two, Kroc was selling milk shake mixers. He had kidney trouble and was drinking too much as he played the piano in the taverns of Chicago. He tried many things-most of which failed-but then became America's most awesome business success. Kroc was an ordinary man and by many standards a failure, when he finally hit his strike with fast food. By the time he was eighty years old, McDonald's had sold its fifty-billionth hamburger. He did it by setting goals and having the initiative and determination to see it to fruition. The best-prepared goals and plans are worthless without that one quality; determination.

One day when I left my home at dawn for an early run, I stopped to stretch at the side of one of the first McDonald's in Northlake, Illinois. I could barely read a plaque through the window of the manager's office. It was a few words, a homily, but it was on target. Here's what it said: "Nothing in the world can take the place of persistence. Talent will not; nothing is more common than unsuccessful men with talent. Genius will not; unrewarded genius is almost a proverb. Education will not; the world is full of educated derelicts. Persistence and determination alone are omnipotent."

This inspirational quote is on the wall of every business I have started. The key element in every individual's success story and of the McDonald Corporation itself, is not luck or good fortune, wealth, or education: it is determination.

Obstacles are in the way of everyone's goals, especially if you are shooting for something really worthwhile. When I hear others say that something is impossible or unlikely to come about, it motivates me. Set your goals and charge ahead without letting fear, anger, or red tape impede your progress. Let other people get stressed while you doggedly attack your goals.

My first business required us to link nine airlines and their reservation computers together. The number of doomsayers was overwhelming. Undauntedly, our team never gave up. One by one, we secured all nine links and launched the first travel agent's computer system into the marketplace.

Since that success, there have been many other business and personal successes in my life. Some acquaintances have said that I am a blessed and fortunate individual. They seem to imply it was all about "luck." I reject that notion. God's blessings are to be respected and appreciated. I have had more than my share, but without my unstinting determination, those qualities would have become mere platitudes. Good fortune favors the determined person.

Write down your goals. Post them somewhere and look at them every day. The answers are all around you. Seek help from others. We all admire determined people. And as Winston Churchill said during the darkest hours of the war, "Never, never, never give up!"

The Christian Road Map to Success: Setting Goals!

Success usually comes to those who are too busy to be looking for it.
Henry David Thoreau

● Prayer

Spend five to fifteen minutes before the start of each day, giving thanks for the blessings God has given you and your family. Then ask for guidance and help to achieve your goals.

● Task

Take three to five steps toward your goal. This initiative will create momentum and like a snowball rolling downhill, it will become an unstoppable force.

Step 1 -

Step 2 -

Step 3 -

Step 4 -

Step 5 -

● Records

Record notes/reflections on the day's accomplishments and results -

● List the most important issue you want to address the next day. Have the phone numbers and contact information ready to go so you can hit the ground running.

● Each day you should read or listen to some positive motivational reinforcement. Provide your mind with some mental nutrition. Consume a balance of motivational and spiritual material. Feed your mind!

● End each day with a prayer of thanks for the blessings God has given you. Ask for His help in achieving your calling. Ask for help in fulfilling God's will.

Everyone who is successful has goals.
Without goals you drift aimlessly like
a boat with no rudder and no direction.

[Principle Ten]
Prayer

Be careful for nothing; but in every thing by prayer and supplication with thanksgiving let your requests be made known unto God.

Philippians 4:6

Prayer is powerful and Americans seem to believe in it. One recent poll says that fifty-six percent of all Americans claim to pray every day. Another seventeen percent say they pray several times each week. Only seven percent say they never pray.[12] The Bible is filled with references to prayer and its positive results. History documents scores and scores of miracles that were a direct result of prayer. Prayer works and God listens to our prayers! Christians call on God intuitively. Even Jesus prayed to His Father in His most trying times.

Pray daily and talk to God every chance you get. Pray big, deep, contemplative prayers. Pray with specificity. Start your prayers giving thanks for all of the blessings God has showered upon you. I suggest that you spend ninety percent of your time in prayer devoted to giving thanks to God. Spend the other ten percent of your time on petitioning the Lord. Sometimes God will answer with a small voice deep inside your soul. Sometimes He will answer by changing your circumstances. Sometimes He will answer by changing you.

---

[12]http://www.foxnews.com/story/0,2933,299374,00.htm

Jesus gave us an example of how to pray when He went into the Garden of Gethsemane. He prayed, meditated, reflected, and prepared Himself for the most important moment in history. We are told His prayer was so intense that He sweated blood. Imagine what would happen if all of us brought that sort of intensity and energy to our own prayer life. I'm guessing that we'd be much better prepared to handle difficult situations. If you read current self-help books, they will teach you that daily mediation, communication with one's self and one's higher power, is the key to success. Authors who want to appeal to the widest possible audience use terms like "source," "meditation," and "higher power." However, make no mistake, only God answers prayers.

Prayer is a powerful tool when dealing with the difficult issues of the day. Prayers to God can help you through troubling times, whether it is family, work, or social situations.

Let me tell you a story about a father who had to kick his son out of the house. The father cared for his oldest son who happened to be adopted. He did more for him than most parents do for their children. He tried to help this young man in a myriad of ways over the years. He may have overcompensated since the boy was adopted. Most importantly, he prayed for his son daily.

Sadly, the son always remained distant from the father; he never called him dad. The son had more problems with the law than most kids-most of them were minor incidents, but he had many of them. As he progressed into his teen years, he accumulated a couple of DUIs, and other petty offenses like public drunkenness, and disturbing the peace. He appeared to have little respect for authority outside the home. Still, his father hoped that he could encourage the young man to change and join the military, or to get a job that was suitable for him.

A few months prior to his twenty-third birthday, the son was assaulted in a gang related incident outside a nightclub. He was beaten unconscious and spent several days in intensive care. He was unable to work for several months while he recuperated at home. His rehabilitation then eased into a lifestyle of lethargy. All he wanted to do was party with his friends. He was a handsome young man and had no problem attracting the attention of women.

One weekend the son returned home on Sunday after a weekend of partying at a hotel with girls. His father asked him to do the dishes. The young man challenged his father's authority for the first time. The father had been patient and tolerated his son's other mistakes. However, when the young man challenged his authority, the father was angry, but restrained his emotions as best he could and did the dishes himself. He made a decision on how to deal with his disrespectful son.

One of the other sons observed what had happened. Although his father didn't yell, he knew that his adopted brother had gone too far by challenging his father's authority as the head of the home. Although the father had not said anything, the younger brother told his older adopted brother, "You better call your friends for a place to stay, because dad is gonna throw you out." That night, the adopted son left without speaking to his father and spent the night somewhere else. The next day while the father was at work, the adopted son returned home to sleep and relax. The father called home and learned that the son had returned home. In a clear and calm voice, the father told the young man that he must vacate the home before he returned from work or he would have the police remove him.

Prayer was an important part of this father's decision. As he washed the dishes, he prayed. The night of the altercation, prior to going to bed, he prayed and forgave his son. The day he arrived at work, he spent twenty minutes in deep contemplative prayer, asking God for guidance. Then he reaffirmed his initial decision, called home, and told his son to leave. The father's conscience was clear. He loved the young man and feared that things would only get worse in the home. His prayers helped to provide him clear thinking in his decision-making.

Prayer should be an essential part of your major decision-making and deliberation process. Seek God's wisdom and grace when you are faced with difficulties, whether it is is family matters or important matters of State.

Perhaps the greatest leader who relied on prayer for support and guidance was the father of our country, George Washington. The story about Washington praying at Valley Forge was recounted by Rev. Nathaniel Snowden, as told to him by eyewitness Isaac Potts, who operated a gristmill in Valley Forge at the time of the Washington's soldiers' encampment.

'I knew personally the celebrated Quaker Potts who saw Gen'l Washington alone in the woods at prayer. I got it from himself, myself. Weems mentioned it in his history of Washington, but I got it from the man myself, as follows:

'I was riding with him (Mr. Potts) in Montgomery County, Penn'a near to the Valley Forge, where the army lay during the war of ye Revolution. Mr. Potts was a Senator in our State & a Whig. I told him I was agreeably surprised to find him a friend to his country as the Quakers were mostly Tories. He said, 'It was so and I was a rank Tory once, for I never believed that America c'd proceed against Great Britain whose fleets and armies covered the land and ocean, but something very extraordinary converted me to the Good Faith!' 'What was that,' I inquired? 'Do you see that woods, & that plain. It was about a quarter of a mile off from the place we were riding, as it happened.' 'There,' said he, 'laid the army of Washington. It was a most distressing time of ye war, and all were for giving up the Ship but that great and good man. In that woods pointing to a close in view, I heard a plaintive sound as, of a man at prayer. I tied my horse to a sapling & went quietly into the woods & to my astonishment I saw the great George Washington on his knees alone, with his sword on one side and his cocked hat on the other. He was at Prayer to the God of the Armies, beseeching to interpose with his Divine aid, as it was ye Crisis, & the cause of the country, of humanity & of the world.

Such a prayer I never heard from the lips of man. I left him alone praying.

'I went home & told my wife. I saw a sight and heard today what I never saw or heard before,

and just related to her what I had seen & heard & observed. We never thought a man c'd be a soldier & a Christian, but if there is one in the world, it is Washington. She also was astonished. We thought it was the cause of God, & America could prevail.' 'He then to me put out his right hand & said 'I turned right about and became a Whig.'

Above all else at Valley Forge Washington held to his faith, and prayer was an essential of his belief-whether vocal in the wooded tract, silent in the stable stall, on bended knee at the bedside or in concert with associates at public service. It is well for men's souls to feel that a leader of men sought and obtained guidance from the Son of Man

Consider This:

● *And he withdrew himself into the wilderness, and prayed.*
  Luke 5:16

● *If the only prayer you said in your whole life was, 'thank you,' that would suffice.*
  Meister Eckhart

● *Do you only pray when in need, or do you give thanks daily for your blessings in a deep and thoughtful way?*

When you pray for another person, you send positive thought energy out to that person via God. I can't explain how it works-that is the mystery of faith. I have used this in my own life and found it really does work. If you are praying for someone, it becomes impossible to feel anger or bitterness toward that individual.

I have prayed with extraordinary results. I had been struggling with my new boss. His style was remarkably different from my previous supervisor. It was tough for me to connect with him. Furthermore, I felt like he did not appreciate what I was doing for the organization. At first, my reaction was to become upset, perturbed, and unmotivated about my job. I internalized everything.

The situation turned around only when I "gave it to God" and began praying for my boss. I asked God to somehow let my boss know that understood my job and was serving to the best of my ability. I also prayed that my boss would receive peace and contentment in his capacity as our organization's leader. I did not pray for myself (although I would have clearly benefited). The results were immediately positive and our relationship improved in a remarkable fashion. Now there is a sense of loyalty and peace in our relationship.

I've been thinking about writing a book for many years, however I was not ready to put these words down on paper. I did not start writing until the Spirit moved me. Now I want to share the positive power of these biblical principles of success with everyone. Of course they are not new. In fact, you and I have heard these principles over the pulpit every Sunday. However, it is not until you reach a certain age of maturity, in my case 40, that these principles begin to take root in your life.

When speaking about prayer, some people like to use the term "meditate." I think the term is limiting and self-centered. Why would you just go into yourself, when you can access the awesome power of our Lord Jesus Christ through prayer? God is listening. He is beyond our comprehension, but He is there. He is there for everyone. He loves us and wants the best for us as His children. He wants us to help others and to be the best people we can be. He has given us the tools and resources to make our lives richer and fuller. In John 10:10, Jesus said, "I am come that they might have life, and that they might have it more abundantly."

I really do believe that old saying that to whom much is given much is expected. For instance, take any of the presidents of the United States in the last thirty years. These gentlemen possessed all of the worldly trappings and all of the power of the strongest nation in the world. Yet much was expected of them. They gave up their privacy to serve our nation. There were those that disagreed with them and disparaged them, no matter what they did. Without exception, all of these humanly-flawed men professed a public faith in God. They turned to God in prayer for guidance in times of crisis and turmoil.

As I confront the many challenges of daily life, I find focused prayer to be very fruitful. God is everywhere and always knows what we need and what we are thinking. In the Bible, over and over again, God makes it clear that if we humble ourselves and seek the Lord, he will answer our prayers.

In 2 Chronicles 7:12, God appeared to Solomon during the night and said to him, "I have heard your prayer... I will hear them from heaven..." When we're engaged in prayer we are actively demonstrating our faith in God.

Jesus said to the two blind men in Matthew 9:29, "Let it [healing] be done according to your faith." They openly petitioned the Lord as He walked by them. This request was granted due to their immense faith in Jesus. The act of prayer is an act of faith and it will be answered. God will always respond to our prayers on His timetable, not ours. Sometimes, no answer is the answer.

The Bible says that the Lord will not give us any burden that we can not handle. Right now, my wife and I are experiencing an emotional roller coaster with the process of trying to adopt our foster children. This has tested our faith. We know God is having us go through this for a reason. We are always looking to find the silver lining. Sometimes we see it and at other times we don't. Nevertheless, I'll admit to that we feel emotionally spent at times. My wife and I have prayed about this issue. We have decided to think positively and act as if the decision on the children has been made and we will be able to keep them. We are acting in faith for the children's future. This has given my wife and me great relief and comfort. We know in our hearts that our Lord will grant us the privilege of raising these beautiful children.

Consider This:

● *Confess your faults one to another, and pray one for another, that ye may be healed. The effectual fervent prayer of a righteous man availeth much.*

James 5:16

● There are no atheists in fox holes.

Anonymous

● *Prayer is exhaling the spirit of man and inhaling the spirit of God.*

Edwin Keith

● *Are you ready to have a continually growing and empowering spiritual dialogue with God and live your life in accordance with his will?*

Application:

● Pray daily.
● Ninety percent of your prayer should be giving thanks.
● Ten percent of your prayer should be for petitions.
● Pray deeply and thoughtfully.
● Pray for others.
● Pray for spiritual-based things that benefit others.
● Recognize that prayers are answered in God's time and not ours, and sometimes no is your answer.
● Use the phrase "Thy will be done" in your prayers.
● Pray for your enemies.

[The Biblical Perspective] *Prayer*

And David spake unto the LORD the words of this song in the day that the LORD
had delivered him out of the hand of all his enemies, and out of the hand of Saul:
And he said, The LORD is my rock, and my fortress, and my deliverer;
The God of my rock; in him will I trust: he is my shield, and the horn of my salvation,
my high tower, and my refuge, my saviour; thou savest me from violence. I will call on
the LORD, who is worthy to be praised: so shall I be saved from mine enemies.
When the waves of death compassed me, the floods of ungodly men made me afraid;
The sorrows of hell compassed me about; the snares of death prevented me;
In my distress I called upon the LORD, and cried to my God: and he did hear my voice
out of his temple, and my cry did enter into his ears.
2 Samuel 22:1-7

The scriptural passage above is the Song of Thanksgiving written by King David to the Lord for rescuing him from his enemies. God chose David to become a king when he was a young shepherd boy and he became one of the greatest kings Israel ever had. God gave David the great responsibility of leading a nation that had many enemies. David knew he could not do it alone and he sought God's help in prayer. David's prayers clearly indicate he had a deep and abiding love for the Lord. There is no doubt that David sinned in his life and did some awful things. Yet, through all of his battles, hardships, ups and downs, and even after he sinned, David always sought the Lord's advice, counsel, guidance, help, and forgiveness. That is why God called David, "a man after mine own heart," in Acts 13:22.

George Washington faced similar challenges when he was burdened with the great weight of leading our fledgling nation. He was overwhelmed and sought the help of God through prayer.

There is something reassuring about knowing that the greatest leaders in history often fall to their knees in prayer during the most trying of times. Although King David and George Washington both commanded vast armies and had many things under their direct control, they still prayed to God for guidance and help. They were also quick to give Him thanks. Praying to God will work for you too! You cannot be a success or have an impact on the world, if you do not pray daily, walk with the Lord, and give him thanks for the shower of blessings He bestows upon you.

Guest Commentary

On Prayer
by Carlton Fulford
Retired General, US Marine Corps

I was blessed by growing up in a Christian home where prayer was a natural part of daily activity. From thanksgiving before meals, to bedtime prayers-communicating with the heavenly Father was both acknowledgment of His Supreme Being as well as a realization of my own frailties and limitations.

As I reflect, the content and character of my prayers have changed over the years. Early in life, my prayers consisted of requests for safety and help in meeting daily challenges. Growing into adulthood, I attained more self-confidence and self-reliance (in truth, overconfidence and arrogance are closer descriptors) and prayers dwindled to an occasional request for guidance in understanding and following God's will. With marriage and children, the need for reliance on God's grace quickly grew and prayers became supplications for the health, welfare, and development of my family as well as wisdom to make the right decisions as a father. As I have gotten older, my prayers have focused more on thanksgiving for the blessings God has given me, concerns for family and friends, and guidance for understanding and fulfilling God's will.

Though intensity, content, and focus have changed over the years-the faith, comfort, and assurance that the Supreme Creator of the universe hears my prayers, cares about me, and will respond to my requests according to His will have provided the foundation for my faith.

Perhaps the most intense times of prayer for me have been those occasions in which I held positions of military leadership or command, during combat.

The responsibility of leading men into combat is immense-arguably one of the most enormous responsibilities of human endeavor. Success or failure on the battlefield is crucial to the overall mission and the responsibility for "life and death" decisions throughout the engagement is all but overwhelming.

Using time wisely in preparing for combat; knowing the strengths and weaknesses of your people and organization; understanding your role and the role of others that you are supporting or who are supporting you; and paying attention to all the details that time and resources will allow are huge responsibilities which are far beyond human capacity to handle alone. That is the significance of such wonderful models as George Washington seeking a quiet sanctuary at Valley Forge and kneeling in the snow to ask for divine guidance before crossing the Delaware River to attack the British.

Once engaged in combat, critical decisions need to be made quickly as events unfold. People on both sides are injured and killed, objectives are taken, and goals are achieved, or you fail. Time does not afford the luxury of contemplation and deep thought. You rely on experience and instinct. Prayers are numerous, but are normally quick and along the lines of: "Lord, help me to do the right thing."

For years after the experience of combat, you find yourself reliving and dealing with the results of your decisions. You question whether you made the right decisions. I have known friends who have experienced great depression over this and were unable to cope with their memories. I have known others who seemingly do not give the matter a second thought. For me, this reflection generates a deeper understanding of my own human frailties, recognition of my need for reliance on a much Higher Being, and a conviction that this Higher Being has forgiven me for my errors along the way. The peace that this conviction affords sustains me each day.

Today, I continue to pray, as a means of communicating with my Maker. I will continue until that glorious day when I will see Him, face-to-face.

[Principle Eleven]
Integrity

Let integrity and uprightness preserve me; for I wait on thee.

Psalm 25:21

We are often told that good guys finish last. Nothing could be farther from the truth.

My friend, Gene Ward is a perfect example of a man of integrity and consistently fine character. Gene was a businessman, intellectual, an quasi-diplomat before he got involved in local politics. Gene was a product of the 1998 Pat Robertson revival within the Republican Party. He was always a gentleman and never forced his beliefs on anyone. However, the media always characterized him as a "religious right-wing Republican."

I first got to know Gene when I was running for the State Legislature in 1994 and then again in 1996. He became my mentor and was like a big brother to me. He called me every day and asked about the progress on my campaign and made sure I was doing all the right things, even though he had his own race. He prayed with me. On Election Day in 1996, I won. The next day I saw him at the Capitol and gave him a big hug. It kind of startled him, but I was so overjoyed with my victory and he was a big part of my win,

That year we had several new Republican party members elected to the State House. Gene was our leader and some wanted to dump him-even some of the guys that he had helped. I was astounded by their lack of loyalty, but thankfully, Gene was re-elected as our minority house leader.

A year later there was a coup in our caucus, and party members wanted to dump Gene in favor of another young, rich, ambitious golden boy who wanted to run for Congress. He figured that Gene's position as minority house leader would benefit him in his future race for Congress. This coup hit Gene hard. It hit me hard. I was naive and could not understand or believe the backstabbing that was taking place. Gene was very disappointed, yet held his head high and carried himself with dignity.

In order to make the best of the situation, Gene used the change in his party's leadership status as an opportunity to pursue a dream he had long contemplated and prayed about. Instead of the headlines reporting that Gene was dumped as leader, they announced that Gene was resigning as house minority leader to run for Congress. Gene became the first announced candidate for Congress and was able to spend time focusing on winning the race. By pushing his own interests, the new minority leader actually made things harder for himself. He sowed the wind and reaped a whirlwind.

Gene began to campaign in earnest. However, the party leadership and hierarchy were not supportive of him because he was an open and devout Christian. Meanwhile, the golden boy also jumped into the race as he had planned all along. He was the favorite of the establishment-the country club Republicans.

Gene worked hard to raise the necessary money for a congressional run-even going so far as to refinance his home. Gene plodded on in a spirit of prayer. The primary election drew close and things continued to appear bleak for Gene. The community, party, and the business establishment supported the opposing Republican candidate. His opponent was way ahead in the polls and Gene's fundraising efforts were starting to stall.

Then the impossible seemed to happen. Gene's Republican opponent quit the race... just dropped out. He checked into a hospital and the doctors said he had high blood pressure. They told him to stop campaigning. He was just

36 years-old at the time, but he effectively left politics and was not heard from for eight years when he again attempted to win the Republican nomination for Congress, but fell short.

After his Republican opponent exited from the 1996 race, Gene immediately became the standard bearer for the party. He went on to win the Republican primary. Unfortunately, he lost in the general election after some vigorous debates with the incumbent Democratic congressman. (Getting elected as a Republican in Hawaii is tough, but Gene ran a good campaign and ran his race with integrity.)

Later, Gene worked for the Bush presidential campaign going door to door in Iowa, Pennsylvania, and other parts of the country. He was rewarded with a presidential appointment at the USAID agency in Washington D.C.

During his congressional campaign, Gene let it slip that someday he would like to become a U.S. ambassador to a foreign country. He reached his dream, just not via the road map he had thought. Gene was appointed the Peace Corps country director in East Timor-helping others to build a better life for themselves, their children, and their communities. After some turmoil in East Timor, Gene returned to Hawaii and ran for his former State House seat and won again in 2006. The outpouring of affection toward Gene was palpable. He continues to serve our community in the State House of Representative.

Gene is revered widely for the way he always carries himself as a gentleman, with dignity and a deep love for the Lord. Gene Ward is a good guy who finishes first!

Consider This:

● *And not only so, but we glory in tribulations also: knowing that tribulation worketh patience; And patience, experience; and experience, hope: And hope maketh not ashamed; because the love of God is shed abroad in our hearts by the Holy Ghost which is given unto us.*

Romans 5:3-5

● *The ultimate measure of a man is not where he stands in moments of comfort and convenience, but where he stands at times of challenge and controversy.*

Martin Luther King, Jr.

● *When others treat you shabbily, does it change your behavior, or do you maintain your integrity?*

Let me tell you about another man I know who has integrity and is a good guy who finished first. Dave Livingston spent 20 years as a YMCA director, mostly in California, then for a short time in Hawaii. During his career as YMCA director, Dave learned a tremendous amount about life and about working with other people. Dave took his extraordinary people skills into the financial planning world and is now a hugely successful stockbroker/financial planner with Edward Jones in Hawaii.

I first meet Dave a few years ago when he was helping a friend of mine run for office. Soon after I got hired by the Navy League, Dave invited me to join him for lunch at the Rotary Club where he was a member. We immediately hit it off. Dave has a great sense of humor and introduced me as "the only guy to ever run for Congress and lose to a dead person." It always got big laughs because although it was true, it is so ridiculously funny.

I could see there was something special about Dave. He was a giver. That day, he spent nearly the entire afternoon, offering help and advice on my new job. He struck me as someone who was successful and wanted me to become successful, too. Dave finds joy in helping others achieve their goals. He reminds me of Jimmy Stewart in the movie, It's a Wonderful Life. You rarely find that quality in people.

Dave has an exhausting schedule. He belongs to several boards and various volunteer organizations. Dave rarely gets more than five hours of sleep as he is often up until 2:30 a.m. communicating to clients and finishing his volunteer work. He also sends out an e-blast at least once a week called, Things Worth Saving. It's a notice of community events that he passes on to others. Dave is continually helping others.

As a result of his hard work and dedication to others, Dave makes six figures a year. In fact he is such a good broker, he is routinely recruited by other financial planning firms and they offer him an even larger salary. He always responds to the headhunters with one question: "What is in it for my clients; what is their net benefit?" This stops the recruiters in their tracks. For Dave, it is not just about filling up his own pockets; he wants what is best for others. This is why Dave's client base keeps growing and growing each year.

Dave has taught me so much. He never goes looking for friends; instead he looks to be a friend and that is why this man of integrity is a good guy who has finishes first.

Integrity is a character trait that is found in most people to varying degrees. However, Dave Livingston and Gene Ward are towers of integrity. Both of these men spend their lives putting other people first.

Consider This:

● *The LORD shall judge the people: judge me, O LORD, according to my righteousness, and according to mine integrity that is in me.*

Psalm 7:8

● *Whatever happens, conduct yourselves in a manner worthy of the gospel of Christ.*

Philippians 1:27

● *The right to do something does not mean that doing it is right.*

William Safire

● *Would you be able to pass up substantial short term rewards for the long-term benefits of others?*

There numerous examples of men of integrity in the Bible. When Nebuchadnezzar, king of Babylon, besieged Jerusalem, the Lord delivered Jehoiakim, king of Judah, to him. As part of his triumph, Nebuchadnezzar ordered that some to the best and brightest of Israel's young men be brought to work for him. These men were to be "blemish free" and were to serve in his palace. In return, they would receive all sorts of training, including the language and literature of the Babylonians. They were offered royal food and wine from the king's table.

Daniel was one of these young Hebrew men and his name meant "God's Justice." Daniel refused to eat from the king's table which had food and wine that was ritualistically offered to Babylon's false gods. He felt that this would defile him and dishonor God. Rather than defile himself, Daniel asked to have nothing but vegetables and water and thereby maintained his integrity. Daniel turned down the pleasure of good food and drink because his personal integrity and relationship with God was far more important to him than the momentary pleasure at the dinner table. Even the king's chief servant was impressed with David. God showed favor on Daniel because he loved and honored Him.

Consider This:

● *But thou, O LORD, be merciful unto me, and raise me up, that I may requite them. By this I know that thou favourest me, because mine enemy doth not triumph over me. And as for me, thou upholdest me in mine integrity, and settest me before thy face for ever. Blessed be the LORD God of Israel from everlasting, and to everlasting. Amen, and Amen.*

Psalm 41:10-13

● *Character is doing the right thing when nobody's looking. There are too many people who think that the only thing that's right is to get by, and the only thing that's wrong is to get caught.*

   J.C. Watts

● *What would you do if a clerk at the supermarket undercharged you?*

Moses is another example of a man with integrity and one of the greatest figures in the Bible. However, Moses was like many of us-we preach a good game, but we don't always live by what we say. There was a time when Moses' integrity was questioned by God. Moses compromised his integrity by living by a different set of rules than the ones he publicly espoused.

God was angry with Moses because he broke God's covenant by not having his son circumcised. Moses' wife immediately corrected this by having their son. Many scholars believe that Moses chose not to circumcise his child because it was not practiced by his wife's culture. No matter the reason, God held Moses personally responsible for keeping His covenant. What Moses chose to ignore is that he was not exempt you from following God's laws just because he was doing God's will in other areas of his life.

When you compromise your integrity, you become personally polluted and you do great harm to yourself. It is like spitting in a clean bucket of water. It makes the entire bucket of water impure. The importance of integrity can not be overstated.

If you walk with God in a path of wholeness and oneness, you will be rewarded. We know this because of what we read in Psalm 41. David, who survived an illness, gave thanks to the Lord. He clearly felt that the Lord healed him from his malady because of his integrity. He also expresses a knowing that this same integrity will allow him to stand in God's presence forever.

Integrity means being "whole," or maintaining a consistent, never wavering set of core values and principles. You have integrity when you say what you mean; mean what you say; and do what you said you would do. We should base all of our relationships on our uncompromising values.

Consider This:

● *If you have integrity, nothing else matters. If you don't have integrity, nothing else matters.*

   Alan Simpson

● *Do you willing put yourself in positions where your integrity will be challenged or compromised?*

Application:

- Act with high moral values in all matters both business and personal, then you will be rewarded.
- Be trustworthy.
- Ask for feedback from those you trust in order to see if you are consistent.
- Honor all commitments and obligations.
- Avoid compromising situations.
- Care about not only the result, but also how it is obtained.
- Display mutual respect to others.
- Act fairly when dealing with others.
- Be an example for others to emulate.

[Principle Twelve]
Forgiveness

For if ye forgive men their trespasses, your heavenly Father will also forgive you: But if ye forgive not men their trespasses, neither will your Father forgive your trespasses.

Matthew 6:14-15

The power to forgive is personally empowering and liberating. Nearly everybody thinks that forgiveness is a good idea. One poll shows that ninety-four percent of Americans believe that forgiveness is important. But in that same survey, only forty-eight percent said that they have actually tried to forgive an offender.[13] So, more than half of the responders found forgiveness so difficult that they weren't even willing to try it.

I had to learn the principle of forgiveness the hard way. During my campaign for Congress, I felt betrayed by leaders in the party and my fellow Republican lawmakers. I carried ill will and anger around inside me for a long time. I admit to making a lot of mistakes during the campaign and I take full responsibility for them.

One of the mistakes is the way I handled my bitterness and those who wronged me. I was immature in my Christian faith and I did not practice forgiveness. In fact, I had a year-long self-pity party after the campaign ended. That's just where I was.

I began my journey of renewal by staying away from politics for a while. I

[13]www.achievesolutions.net/achievesolutions/en/nchealthchoice/Content.do?contentId=9215

read self-help books and listened to motivational tapes. What an emotional cleanser! As I released the baggage of bitterness and moved closer to God, I began to laugh about my experiences during the congressional race. When people would ask me about the campaign, I would launch into a funny story about how I messed up and I could genuinely laugh. I was liberated. Christ enabled me to turn extreme disappointment into humor. I was touched by the Holy Spirit and since then I refuse to let anyone continue to hurt me. I will not allow myself to be eaten up by negative rhetoric anymore. Instead I have asked God to forgive them. I chose to release the bitterness and hurt to God and let him deal with the wrong doer. It worked! My job is to forgive them, learn from the experience, and move forward.

Forgiving others is a principle that Jesus explicitly taught and modeled. In His moments of pain and despair on the cross, he asked God to forgive the perpetrators for they knew not what they did. How remarkable was that? At no time in our life will we be asked to mimic the passion of the Christ, however, we have daily opportunities to practice forgiveness on a much more mundane level. Sometimes forgiving others is difficult. There is a temptation to relive the slights, insults, or wrongs and stew about them. Of course, this behavior is a dead-end street that only causes more internal turmoil and ill feelings. Carrying a grudge or failing to forgive is unproductive and can hurt you mentally and physically.

When you forgive others, you feel empowered and liberated. You can take charge of your emotions by releasing the issue to God. The process allows you to move forward with a free and untroubled spirit.

Consider This:

● *And be ye kind one to another, tenderhearted, forgiving one another, even as God for Christ's sake hath forgiven you.*

Ephesians 4:32

● *Forgiveness is the fragrance that the violet sheds on the heal that has crushed it.*

  Mark Twain

● *When you are slighted or wronged, do you hold a grudge, or practice immediate forgiveness?*

I shared ideas with a colleague in hopes of giving him an opportunity to work with me on an important high-profile project. My motivations were genuine. I later followed up by emailing him an electronic file of the plan for his comment and review. After not receiving a timely response, I called him and inquired if he was still interested in working together. I was surprised to learn that he took credit for my ideas and was working on it on his own.

Initially I was angry, then I thought about how I could make something positive out of this situation. I then suggested that we work on two versions of the idea and bring synergy to this important project. He agreed.

I had a choice to make. I could have gotten angry and chewed him out and belittled him. Instead I chose to focus on the positive aspects of the situation. I was upset for about five minutes, but then I let it go.

This kind of stuff happens every day. We need to take such slights with a grain of salt and forgive. Choose to build relationships with forgiveness rather than tearing them down with bitterness and forgiveness. Forgiveness sets you free.

Consider This:

● *Then came Peter to him, and said, Lord, how oft shall my brother sin against me, and I forgive him? till seven times? Jesus saith unto him, I say not unto thee, Until seven times: but, Until seventy times seven.*

  Matthew 18:21-22

● *To forgive is to set a prisoner free and discover the prisoner was you.*

   Unknown

● *Am I not destroying my enemies when I make friends of them?*

   Abraham Lincoln

● *Do you look for ways to mend fences, or do you look for retribution?*

Application:

● Remit the offense to God. Give it to him to bear.

● Release the offender and the offense to the Lord.

● Release your attachment to the pain.

● Refrain from retaliation. It only creates more heartache.

● Learn from slights and offenses.

● Avoid situations where offense by others is likely.

● Ask the Holy Spirit for strength in the forgiveness process.

● Pray for your offender during the forgiveness process.

● Seek a pastor or priest when stuck in unforgiveness.

● Take responsibility for your part of the dispute, recognize any slights you have may committed, and ask for forgiveness quickly.

The Biblical Perspective: *Forgiveness*

The servant therefore fell down, and worshiped him, saying, Lord, have patience with me, and I will pay thee all. Then the lord of that servant was moved with compassion, and loosed him, and forgave him the debt. But the same servant went out, and found one of his fellow servants, which owed him an hundred pence: and he laid hands on him, and took him by the throat, saying, Pay me that thou owest. And his fellowservant fell down at his feet,

[The Biblical Perspective] *Forgiveness*

The servant therefore fell down, and worshiped him, saying, Lord, have patience with me, and
I will pay thee all. Then the lord of that servant was moved with compassion, and loosed him,
and forgave him the debt. But the same servant went out, and found one of his fellow servants,
which owed him an hundred pence: and he laid hands on him, and took him by the throat,
saying, Pay me that thou owest. And his fellow servant fell down at his feet, and besought
him, saying, Have patience with me, and I will pay thee all. And he would not: but went and
cast him into prison, till he should pay the debt. So when his fellow servants saw what was
done, they were very sorry, and came and told unto their lord all that was done. Then his
lord, after that he had called him, said unto him, O thou wicked servant, I forgave thee all
that debt, because thou desiredst me: Shouldest not thou also have had compassion on thy
fellow servant, even as I had pity on thee? And his lord was wroth, and delivered him to the
tormentors, till he should pay all that was due unto him. So likewise shall
my heavenly Father do also unto you, if ye from your hearts forgive not every
one his brother their trespasses.
Matthew 18:26-35

We must forgive others who have sinned against us, or wronged us in some manner. In the parable of the unforgiving servant, Jesus commanded that we forgive others for their offenses, as He has forgiven us. The unforgiving servant asked his master to be forgiven his debt—and was. However, the servant that had been forgiven did not have compassion on another fellow servant that owed him money. The fellow servant asked for more time to pay. He had the follow servant thrown in prison for failing to pay his debt. The Lord says that we will receive the same treatment that we offer our debtors. Quite simply, if we forgive others we will be forgiven. However, if we have hard hearts and refuse to forgive others, we should expect the same treatment from our Heavenly Father.

Most successful people in the business world are forgivers. They are too busy to hold grudges and hard feelings against those who have injured them. Make no mistake, they have not forgotten, but they have granted forgiveness. In fact, once forgiveness is conferred, their head and heart are clear of negative emotions that may cloud their judgment. That makes them free to analyze the past experience so they can learn valuable lessons from it. This is how forgiveness contributes to success.

Forgiveness is vitally important in our homes. Husbands and wives must forgive each other and their children all of the time. If family members have hardened hearts like the unforgiving debtor, then they will not be a close family. On the other hand, if they practice forgiveness daily, as the Lord does with us, they will find that their home is a place filled with acceptance, love, and peace.

Since God has forgiven us, the least we can do to forgive others. True forgiveness is an act of love.

Guest Commentary

Jesslyn McManus
Interview about Forgiveness
McManus is with The Institute for the Psychological Sciences[14]

Many would agree that it is good to forgive one's enemies, and that forgiveness contributes to mental health. So why is it sometimes difficult to let go of anger or hatred toward those who have hurt us?

In recent years, forgiveness has come to be seen by many as an effective means to bring about psychological healing to those who are suffering from the effects of an injustice. Anger, whether outwardly expressed or defensively denied, is a reoccurring theme in psychotherapy.

Forgiveness therapy models, such as those offered by Robert Enright and Richard Fitzgibbons, E. Worthington, and F. DiBlasio, offer an alternative to common methods for dealing with anger and resentment, which rely primarily upon expression and/or the use of medication.

Forgiveness therapy is used in order to help people gradually let go of resentment and hatred, which causes stress and psychological pain. After working through each of the phases in the "forgiveness model," the client is able to make a moral response of goodness toward the offender.

However, when anger and hatred come to take on a central role in one's life, problems may arise even when one has successfully worked through the forgiveness stages and the dispositions are abandoned. These difficulties, which may become apparent in "post-forgiveness therapy," need to be addressed with empathy, genuine care, and skillful guidance.

---

[14]Interview 9/10/2006 www.catholiconline.com

Given its vivacious quality, hatred has a powerful attraction which is difficult to resist. Although forgiveness contributes to mental health, it is sometimes difficult to let go of anger or hatred toward those who have hurt us because of the psychological "benefits" these emotional states provide.

Pain or hurt is usually underlying anger or hatred. Therefore, hatred can be seen as a way to protect oneself from damage to one's self-image or concept. However, these "rewards," which are associated with egocentric gratification, only perpetuate hatred and impede psychological and spiritual health.

What kinds of psychological benefits does hatred provide on a short-term basis that makes it difficult to let go of?

As psychologists Paul Vitz and Philip Mango point out, hatred can be used to defend against painful memories and emotions. As long as one hates, he or she does not have to confront or experience the underlying pain and suffering caused by the offender. It also keeps one from recognizing that one's self is flawed and that others have positive attributes.

In addition, hatred may become so pronounced that it comes to provide a sense of meaning or purpose in one's life and makes one feel alive and powerful. In cases where intense hatred persists over a long period of time, it may also come to serve as a means of self-identification.

A person may come to define himself in a negative way, by contrasting himself with the one he hates. Those who find themselves in this situation may experience an existential crisis and psychological pain manifested in the form of profound feelings of emptiness, upon letting go of the hatred.

What is it about our postmodern culture that leads people to latch onto hatred for a sense of identity, and how can a person move toward an accurate sense of self devoid of negative attitudes?

In its forms of deconstruction as well as its rejection of universal truths, postmodern culture produces a society in which "knowing oneself" proves to be a difficult task.

The absence of tradition and shared meaning and values characteristic of postmodern society has resulted in a fragile, empty sense of self. This condition leads people to turn to such things as consumerism to fill the vacant self as Phillip Cushman states.

This lack of rootedness, combined with a fragmented sense of reality, makes it difficult for one to establish a firm sense of where one came from and who one is today. This sets up a context in which self-identification through hatred will flourish.

A person can move toward an accurate sense of self devoid of negative attitudes by fulfilling their vocation as relational beings, who are... made for love.

What is the next step, after letting go of anger and hatred? What is the significance of "filling the void"?

As was previously stated, successful removal of the hatred may produce an existential void and the loss of sense of self. The hatred must be replaced with something engendering self-worth, namely, altruism-that is, living a life of true Christian charity.

The next step after letting go of anger and hatred, therefore, is to redefine oneself as a person who loves rather than one who hates, through acts of self-giving. The significance of "filling the void" is to provide the person with newfound meaning in their lives and a source of identity through love.

In what sense do you equate altruistic activities with the virtue of Christian charity, or love?

Both altruism and Christian love involve self-giving, moving away from the self and toward others. This love was perfectly exemplified in Christ Jesus.

How has altruistic behavior proven successful in improving mental health?

Many studies have shown that altruistic emotions and behaviors are associated with psychological health and well-being. In his article "Altruism, Happiness and Health: It's Good to be Good," Stephen Post provides a summary of the literature in this area.

Some of the factors which have been found to help bring about these psychological benefits are enhanced social integration, distraction from the agent's own problems, increased perception of self-efficacy and competence, and enhanced meaningfulness.

On what level could secular psychology adopt this theory, and how does our Catholic faith imbue it with a deeper dimension?

This theory may be formalized in a clinical program in which self-giving love is actualized in overt altruistic acts. This therapeutic program may be implemented once the forgiveness process is under way.

The program would resemble the following:

The client would be encouraged to choose a person whom the client feels is having a difficult time and is need of care, and to do specific acts of kindness for him or her. This may consist of running an errand, cooking a meal, or simply calling the individual often to see how he or she is doing.

In addition, the client will be asked to choose a secondary group or organization to which he can offer his time. For example, the person may choose to volunteer at a soup kitchen, visit the elderly in a nursing home, or work with disabled children.

They will keep a journal in order to track their progress in their altruistic activities. They will record what each act was and for whom each was done. They should also include the feelings they experience and any feedback they receive.

While these acts may not be altruistic in the true sense of the word in the beginning-since they are done as part of a therapeutic program-they will lead the client to understand the merit of living selflessly. This will, in turn, lead the person to do truly altruistic acts on his or her own initiative as time goes on.

Theologically, the idea that people are fulfilled in and through community with others is based on the idea that we are created in the image and likeness of a triune God whose very being is self-giving love. Therefore, this type of program would not only be effective in that it would bring about psychological benefits for the client. It also would enable people to fulfill their vocation as persons made for self-giving and relationships with others.

Furthermore, in helping others to cultivate the virtue of charity, the therapist plays a role in bringing about the kingdom of God on earth.

The power to forgive
is personally empowering and liberating.
You can take charge of your emotions
by releasing the issue to God. The process
allows you to move forward with
a free and untroubled spirit.

[Principle Thirteen]
Initiative

There cometh a woman of Samaria to draw water: Jesus saith unto her, Give me to drink.
(For his disciples were gone away unto the city to buy meat.) Then saith the woman of
Samaria unto him, How is it that thou, being a Jew, askest drink of me, which am a woman of
Samaria? for the Jews have no dealings with the Samaritans. Jesus answered and said unto
her, If thou knewest the gift of God, and who it is that saith to thee, Give me to drink; thou
wouldest have asked of him, and he would have given thee living water.

John 4:7-10

In the preceding scripture passage, Jesus displayed initiative in speaking to the Samaritan woman. Samaria was located between Judea and Galilee. Due to animosity between the Jews and Samaritans, Jews would rather take a longer route to avoid passing through Samaria and have any contact with Samaritans. Further Jewish men didn't speak publicly to women, and would have no dealing with a woman with poor reputations. However Jesus had a mission. He purposely traveled to Samaria and stopped at Jacob's well, weary and thirsty. The Samaritan woman came at a time of day when she wouldn't have to be confronted by others that would heckle or snub her due to her immoral lifestyle. Jesus asked the Samaritan woman for a drink of water. The woman was taken aback that a Jewish man would speak to her. However, Jesus took the initiative to take the conversation to a higher level and tell her about the gift of God, living water, and the way to salvation. He was not overbearing, but subtle and thought-provoking which caused the Samaritan woman to thirst for the gift of the living water--Jesus. In the end many Samaritans also believed in Jesus because of the woman's testimony. None of this would have happened if Jesus hadn't take initiative to go to Samaria to speak to this woman. This story demonstrates the power of initiative to create positive change.

Initiative is in the Boy Scout's oath, preached in the Marine Corps, and in every successful organization. Self-help experts like Tony Robbins have written entire books concerning the issue. However, it is really quite simple. Like the Nike slogan says: "Just do it!" Get off your duff and take action.

Everything starts with a thought. God has given you the intelligence and gifts to be able to accomplish almost anything. As I write this, I am forty-three years-old, married with a family, and many responsibilities. However, if I decided to become a doctor, I could. I would just have to make certain changes in my life, and go back to school to get the proper training. I probably couldn't become a professional athlete at this stage of my life because the laws of nature limit what I can do physically. However, mentally and spiritually, you and I can do anything with the awesome help of God.

What is it that you want to do? Do you have the courage to make the decision to pursue it? If so, take bold and decisive actions. Each day, take a step or create movement toward your goal and you will create an unstoppable momentum. Before you know it, your will have built momentum, a tidal wave of energy. The key to whatever you want to do is to start! Take that small step in the right direction and keep going.

Riki Ellison is the living embodiment of initiative. Riki was a former pro football player with the San Francisco 49ers during their glory years. Riki wanted our country to be protected from rouge nations that acquire missiles. He saw a vacuum and decided to fill it. Where there was nothing, he created something. He set a goal, took action.

In 2002, he founded Missile Defense Advocacy Alliance (MDAA), the leading non-profit organization educating and advocating for the development and deployment of effective missile defense systems. This vital work is protecting our nation and families from ballistic missiles. Under his continued leadership, MDAA has grown to more than 9,000 members across the U.S.

I attended a briefing by MDAA presented by Riki. After the briefing, people crowded around Riki, introducing themselves and telling him who they are and what they do. His eyes glazed over with a disinterested, yet polite look. (I have observed this happening often in life whenever a celebrity or a famous person is introduced to others.)

Finally, I took the initiative to speak to him. I said, "How can I help you?" You should have seen his surprise. He was immediately very interested in me. Based on his response, I was able to help him by setting up a MDAA briefing at our local veterans' center. In return, he gave me twenty invitations to a private dinner briefing at an upscale hotel. We were able to mutually help each other. By exercising initiative, I got so much more in return.

I think God has shown Riki's life favor because giving back to the community is an important part of his life. Riki was the head coach of T.C. Williams High School in Alexandra Virginia, portrayed in the movie, "Remember the Titans." He did this without pay. As he said it was all about "helping kids."

Riki's biggest project took form in 2005 with Youth Impact Program that reaches out to at-risk youth. The program founded by Riki was created with the support of the University of Southern California Joint Education Program and the National Football Youth Football Fund and the Los Angeles Technical College. The program has now been successful for three years at USC, with more than two hundred boys aged nine to twelve enrolled in a rigorous program focusing on academics, life skills and athletics.

In 2008, the Youth Impact Program expanded to New Orleans and Ellison is currently working toward his goal to have every major city involved with this program. Inner city at risk youth in Philadelphia, Detroit, and Cleveland will benefit from this program in the near future.

Once Riki makes a decision, he exercises initiative and takes action, his efforts are unstoppable. Likewise, when we use initiative we should be working to serve others and bring about positive change, to make the world a better place. If your motivations are good and this is the "right" thing for you to be doing, God will help you. If not, He will withhold His help.

Consider This:

● *You don't have to be great to start, but you have to start to be great.*

Zig Ziglar

● *One of the best ways to get others to help you is by offering to help them. Do you exercise this sort of positive initiative?*

My parents told me I needed to get a college degree. I also knew that God wanted me to go to college. However, it was up to me to apply for admission, complete the financial aid forms, and find a place to live, etc.

When I decided to get involved in politics and run for office, I just did it! Contrary to popular thought, political machines really do not exist and do not "groom" candidates to run for office. It is a grueling process and you have to take the initiative and put yourself in the arena. You must go door to door on your own, you must raise money, and all of the other things associated with politics. No one is going to hold your hand. You need to do it. The challenges are rewarding because you know your initiative and energy created the dynamic event called a campaign.

In the Marine Corps, initiative is highly valued. In fact, Marines are even rated in their performance evaluations on their ability to display initiative.

This is important because someday a Marine may find himself leading others under heavy fire and he must take decisive action for the others to survive.

In the business world, initiative is critical. Currently, I run the Navy League in Honolulu, where I use my God-given initiative all of the time. I must raise interest by educating government officials and the general public about key maritime issues and the importance of a capable and prepared sea services to secure America's future. In addition our organization provides support to the service men and women in the sea services and their families. Raising funds is another area of my responsibility. As head of the organization I am responsible to ensure that we perform the administrative work at the highest level. Recently, I copied all of our important files to a CD-Rom so that we would have copies of our organizations by-laws, IRS letters, and other important documents. No one told me to do this, but I saw a need and took action.

Some of my most rewarding moments have come about because of initiative. Our fundraising event in which Senator John McCain was our keynote speaker was hugely successful because of my God-inspired initiative. I firmly believe that God helped us secure this respected and sought-after speaker. God allowed McCain to clear his schedule and take a ten-hour flight to Hawaii and turn around the next day for another ten-hour trip back to Washington D.C. This sort of thing does not happen unless God is involved.

Consider This:

● *What then shall we say to these things? If God is for us, who can be against us?*
  Romans 8:31

● *Time is neutral and does not change things. With courage and initiative, leaders change things.*
  Jesse Jackson

● *I would rather regret the things I have done than the things I have not.*

    Lucille Ball

● *Be willing to make decisions--that's the most important quality in a good leader. Don't fall victim to what I call the ready-aim-aim-aim-aim syndrome. You must be willing to fire.*

    T. Boone Pickens

● *Do you have a project or dream that you've always wanted to pursue, but never have? What is stopping you from starting to work on it right now?*

Application:

● Ask God for guidance regarding your dreams.

● Write down your dreams and goals, then prioritize them.

● Take action every day toward your goals.

● Be creative and think "outside of the box"... with God, anything is possible.

● Help others who are chasing their own dreams.

● Be bold.

● Be enthusiastic about your ideas.

[Principle Fourteen]
Humility

Whosoever therefore shall humble himself as this little child,
the same is greatest in the kingdom of heaven.

Matthew 18:4

A few years ago I went for a haircut at the Navy Exchange in Pearl Harbor. I waited about forty-five minutes in a long line. I had my number from the numbering system and I was next in the queue. I saw a barber become free. Instead of being next, he motioned for someone behind me. I was steamed! As I sat waiting for the next barber, I grew even angrier. I looked over at the barber who slighted me and I noticed that he was talking to the young man in the chair in a foreign language. It became quite clear that they were family.

I felt ashamed of myself. How petty could I be to begrudge a hard working barber the opportunity to do his family member a favor? I know I would not want to be a barber. It is hard work and you are on your feet all day. I felt sorry for him. It really put things in perspective for me. I was the lucky one, even though I got skipped over and had to wait a little longer.

Real humility is a character trait that will enable you to glide through life with much less stress than you would normally have to bear. Leave your ego at the door. It is baloney and inconsistent with Christianity. Most of the time when we feel insulted, slighted, or wronged, there is inflated self-importance at work. God's word tells that the proud will be humbled and those that are humble will be exalted.

I'm not talking about abandoning genuine self-confidence and self-esteem. On the contrary-you should feel good about yourself because you were created in the image of Christ. You are special and so is every other human being you encounter in your daily journey.

Consider This:

● *I tell you, this man went down to his house justified rather than the other: for every one that exalteth himself shall be abased; and he that humbleth himself shall be exalted.*

Luke 18:14

● *Egotism is the anesthetic that dulls the pain of stupidity.*

Frank Leahy

● *Do you come off arrogant and demanding to others? Are you considered pushy?*

Your job is what puts food on the table, but it is not who you are. Working for a job title so that we can feel validated leads to emptiness. For the first forty-one years of my life, I found my identity in my profession and was always's chasing society's approval. Right out of high school I earned the title of Marine. I thought I was special because of that accomplishment. Then I went to college and got my bachelors degree-a prerequisite for validation in today's society. Then I re-enlisted and became a Marine Corps officer. After leaving the Corps I went back to school to get my MBA degree-a required credential in the upper echelons of business. When movement in the business world became too slow, I ran for public office-the ultimate public validation experience. However, these accomplishments never gave me the validation I was looking for. Eventually, I found validation in who I am in Christ.

No titles, achievements, or any other earthly placards of success should define us. We are all equal and special in God's eyes. When you truly understand that we are all bothers and sisters in Christ, then you will look at people differently.

I already told you about my fall from grace in the political world. Afterwards, I struggled to find work, but thankfully I eventually found a job with a security agency. Going from an elected official to a security guard was a huge blow to my ego. The Lord served me-and rightly so-a giant piece of humble pie! My kids observed this huge fall in status, but I was grateful to be employed and made light of the situation. I think they learned a lesson while observing me going through it all. Today, I thank God for that humbling experience, for it has made me a better man.

To paraphrase scripture, he who humbles himself as a servant to all is the greatest among men. Jesus is the perfect example. He is God yet He came and submitted Himself to a terrible death that was humiliating and brutal. Philippians 2:8 says: "And being found in fashion as a man, he humbled himself, and became obedient unto death, even the death of the cross." His passion was an act of love and humility. If Jesus could go through that for us, what should we be prepared to do for our fellow man?

Consider This:

● *Humble yourselves therefore under the mighty hand of God, that he may exalt you in due time: Casting all your care upon him; for he careth for you.*

   Psalm 25:9

● *It is not titles that honor men, but men that honor titles.*

   Niccolo Machiavelli

● *Do you treat all people with respect and dignity that they are entitled to as children of God?*

The last story is about the effects of pride. "Mel" and I and worked for the same company in different divisions, about fifteen years ago. We are about the same age, had a lot in common, and became friends. We were both on the bottom rung of the corporate ladder. We maintained contact on and off after we left the company.

Mel was driven by financial success and became quite wealthy. He married a professional woman who makes a great mid-six figure living as well. Today, his net worth is in the millions. That is a tremendous leap from where he was fifteen years ago when we were both starting out in our respective careers.

Nothing is wrong with becoming wealthy if it is done with the right motives-to help others and make the world a better place. Sadly, in the last five years, his behavior is disturbing to the point that I don't want to be around him anymore. He is consumed by the material world and he has lost focus on the real meaning of life. It seems that as Mel's wealth has increased, his regard for others has decreased. I have watched him treat restaurant wait staff and business service providers with rudeness and disrespect. Long-term friends were exiled to the ash heap because they had a minor disagreement.

Society was partly to blame for his downfall as well. As Mel acquired more and more wealth, people gave him preferential treatment. He received perks and gifts from those looking to curry favor from him. Apparently, Mel was not sufficiently grounded and allowed this treatment to go to his head.

The ironic thing about humility is the more that you practice it, the greater the likelihood that you will be admired and "lifted up" by your family, friends, and colleagues. This trait will enable you to be much more successful in your personal and professional life.

Consider This:

● *A man's pride shall bring him low: but honour shall uphold the humble in spirit.*

Proverbs 29:23

● *None are so empty as those who are full of themselves.*

   Benjamin Whichcote

● *Humility is the only certain defense against humiliation.*

   Anonymous

● *Are you grounded enough to withstand a windfall of success, wealth, and fame? Would you still be humble?*

Application:

● Be courteous and respectful of others at all times.
● Be confident in your abilities and demeanor-yet humble.
● Put other people's needs first.
● Refrain from gossip and self-righteous judgment of others.
● Do not criticize in the spirit of being a "helper."
● Control your temper.
● Reconcile with your foes.
● Pray for others.
● Draw attention to the success of others.
● Serve the least among us, as Jesus did.
● Praise others often and genuinely.

[The Biblical Perspective] *Humility*

And Pilate asked him, saying, Art thou the King of the Jews? And he answered him
and said, Thou sayest it. Then said Pilate to the chief priests and to the people,
I find no fault in this man.
Luke 23:3-4

Jesus Christ serves as the ultimate example of humility. Jesus is God, yet He surrendered all of His privileges and humbled himself to come to earth as a man. Jesus was without sin—the only perfect human to ever walk the earth. Yet, He had no pride or egocentric thoughts as evidenced in the powerful scriptural passage above.

In this passage, Pilate asked Jesus (who is God incarnate), if He was the king of the Jews. Jesus answer was humble and so disarming. Jesus could have defended himself and could have done miracles to humble Pilate and all the others who questioned him. Acts 8:32 says: "He was led as a sheep to the slaughter; and like a lamb dumb before his shearer, so opened he not his mouth...." Jesus knew that He had a mission to fulfill: to die on the cross and suffer for all of mankind's sins so they could be forgiven. He was the greatest among us, yet a servant who came as ransom for our sins.

Pilate could not find any fault in Jesus and was baffled about what to do with him. Pilate turned back to the Jews and said he could find no guilt in this man. Jesus was falsely accused. However, to appease the Jewish leaders and people, Jesus was beaten, tortured, humiliated, and crucified on the cross. Jesus never lost his composure and remained humble and dignified.

Philippians 2:7-9 says: "Who, being in the form of God, thought it not robbery to be equal with God: But made himself of no reputation, and took upon him the form of a servant, and was made in the likeness of men: And being found in fashion as a man, he humbled himself, and became obedient unto death, even the death of the cross. Wherefore God also hath highly exalted him, and given him a name which is above every name...." Jesus was exalted because He humbled himself as a servant and chose to die on the cross for our sins.

When I reflect on what Jesus did, I also think of Dr. Martin Luther King, Jr. He battled for civil rights based on his Christian faith. King was beaten, spit on, and cursed; yet he remained humble and dignified. His example was Christ Jesus.

In turn, if you live your life for others, in a humble fashion, you will find success beyond your wildest dreams. The greatest among us must be willing to serve the least among us, because those who much is given, much is expected. (Luke 12:48)

Guest Commentary

On Humility
by David A. Pendleton
Judge and Former Hawaii State Legislator

"No one likes a show-off," said my grandmother, commenting on my overly triumphant and less than humble win in a chess game against my younger brother. I was nine and he was seven. I was engaging in all the post-tackle posturing for which football players get cited as being unsportsmanlike.

"Egomaniacs do," I said without pause, showcasing a new word recently acquired from my dad. I thought I was being smart.

"No, egomaniacs love themselves excessively," Grandmother said. "That's why no one likes them either."

She was right-again.

Likability aside, there is a reason why we cringe in the presence of those who are boastful. We know instinctively that there is something wrong with bragging. It is no wonder that the Bible has a lot to say about the sin of pride and the virtue of humility.

Pride goes before destruction and haughtiness before a fall.
Proverbs 16:18, TLB

Pride ends in a fall, while humility brings honor.
Proverbs 29:23, TLB

You younger men, follow the leadership of those who are older. And all of you serve each other with humble spirits, for God gives special blessings to those who are humble, but sets Himself against those who are proud. If you will humble yourselves under the mighty hand of God, in His good time He will lift you up. (1 Peter 5:5-6, TLB)

Pride can cut us off from God and from others. Pride is what caused the devil to seek to compare himself with God. Pride is what has gotten humankind in the trouble it is in today. The Genesis narrative of Adam and Eve describes the first temptation as involving a prideful desire to be like God.

If excessive pride can sour one's relationship with God, then its opposite, the virtue of humility, can nourish one's relationship with God. "Therefore anyone who humbles himself as this little child is the greatest in the Kingdom of Heaven" (Matthew 18:4, TLB).

St. Theresa of Avila once observed that "by meditating upon His humility we find how very far we are from being humble." She was right, of course. When we keep our eyes on Christ, the rest of life comes into focus.

Being humble does not mean being a spineless person-always acceding to the demands of others. Humility does not mean having a negative view of oneself. It does not mean entertaining a low sense of self-esteem.

On the contrary, genuine humility means seeing ourselves through the eyes of God-recognizing that our talents come from God and are loaned to us to serve others. It means loving people, not by our own superficial standards, but as God loves them. Humility means remembering that all that we have and all that we are comes from God.

Real humility
is a character trait that
will enable you. Leave
your ego at the door.
God tells us the proud
will be humbled and
the humble will be exalted.

[Principle Fifteen]
Faith

But without faith it is impossible to please him: for he that cometh to God must believe that he is, and that he is a rewarder of them that diligently seek him.

Hebrews 11:6

When I was going through Marine Corps Officer candidate school, I prayed a lot. I had to rely on God to pull me through. I was newly married, less than a year, and we had an infant son. I was deeply in love with my wife and little boy. As I arrived and settled in for training, the reality that I would be separated from them for three months began to sink in.

I was also hurting physically. I never felt such despair in my life. I sat quietly on my foot locker looking at my wife's picture with tears rolling down my face. I was homesick, depressed, and I missed my wife terribly. The feeling of loss was so great that I felt part of my body was missing. To top it all off, I was in the midst of Marine Corps officer training with a badly sprained ankle. I had injured it week prior to my departure, but kept this a secret because I had already passed my physical.

I learned a lot about myself at OCS. I learned that I had a big mouth and was my own worst enemy at times. I barely made it through the program. During the ninth week, I was forced to see the Colonel because of my bad attitude. I took responsibility for my big mouth and admitted all of my mistakes. I promised to change and become a better Marine. The willingness to admit that I was wrong, take responsibility for my actions, and pledge to be a better Marine saved me.

During this whole ordeal, I prayed for guidance. This is where faith came into the picture. I knew in my heart that I was not going to be thrown out before graduation. My prayers were answered and I went on to graduate and become a United States Marine Corps officer-thanks to the power and the glory of God's protective hand.

Nothing is impossible with God's help. He can cure your illnesses and answer your prayers, according to His will. The God we have is a loving God who wants the best for His children. He will show you favor if you believe in Him, love Him, and ask for His help.

Consider This:

● That Christ may dwell in your hearts by faith; that ye, being rooted and grounded in love.

Ephesians 3:17

● *It is true that every day has its own evil, and its good too. But how difficult must life be, especially farther on when the evil of each day increases as far as worldly things go, if it is not strengthened and comforted by faith. And in Christ all worldly things may become better, and, as it were, sanctified. Theo, woe is me if I do not preach the Gospel; if I did not aim at that and possess faith and hope in Christ, it would be bad for me indeed, but no I have some courage.*

Vincent van Gogh

● *You can do very little with faith, but you can do nothing without it.*

Samuel Butler

● *When you have done all you can do, how do you handle situations that are beyond your control?*

The greatest testing and confirming time of faith comes when a loved one is facing death. My father was gravely ill and dying of cirrhosis of the liver. I did my crying before I went to see him because I wanted to present a calm and reassuring presence. It was just the two of us in the hospital room at 3:00 in the morning. It was dark and cool. Death loomed at the door. We both knew that he was going to die in the next few hours. Despite this, my father was extraordinarily coherent and his mind was still sharp, but his body had given out after years of alcohol abuse. We talked about his impending departure from this world as if he were getting ready to board an airplane for a far off destination. I asked him if he was afraid to die. Dad said he was a little scared, but ready.

Despite his past sins, I knew that Dad belonged to Jesus Christ. He had asked for forgiveness a few days earlier and this had a peaceful effect on both of us. We both had faith in God and the assurance that God was going to take him home.

While holding Dad's hand in his last hours, it became clear to me that dying is indeed part of living. We all die. Faith in Christ is our only salvation, but what a joyous salvation it is! I continued to comfort him and held his hand until he passed. When he stopped breathing, he gave up the ghost and his body became an empty shell. I did not weep over his body, because I knew that his soul and was still alive. Dad's soul left his body and he was in God's hands.

Let me share another example of faith. A young woman, "Jill" learned that her dad had cancer two weeks before Christmas. By the first week in January, his condition had worsened. He could not swallow because of a hole in his esophagus, so they tried to close it up by putting a metal tube in his throat, but that did not work. One morning around 2:00 a.m. her mom had to take him to the emergency room. He could not swallow his own saliva and had to spit into a cup instead. He received temporary treatment and was released later that day and returned home. Later that week, Jill had to take him to the hospital again because his condition worsened. It was the beginning of the worst week in her life. She was at the hospital from 6:00 a.m. to 3:00 a.m. Then she returned to her home, got a little sleep, and started it all over again.

The night before he died, her family had a bedside service. Their pastor came and led the family in a time of prayer. The pastor encouraged Jill to say a few words because she was close to her dad. Jill could not speak and started crying. Then the Holy Spirit came over her and the words flowed out of her mouth. The Lord enabled her to say comforting words for the whole family. When her father passed away, the family was relieved because his suffering was over and he was going to a better place.

Consider This:

● *His lord said unto him, Well done, thou good and faithful servant: thou hast been faithful over a few things, I will make thee ruler over many things: enter thou into the joy of thy lord.*

Matthew 25:21

● *This is all the inheritance I can give my dear family. The religion of Christ can give them one which will make them rich indeed.*

The Last Will and Testament of Patrick Henry

● *He who loses money, loses much; He who loses a friend, loses much more; He who loses faith, loses all.*

Eleanor Roosevelt

As the previous two stories show, most of us rely on faith in times of death and sickness. We are instinctively and intuitively drawn to that well of comfort, knowing that there is a higher power called God. We often forget about our faith in God and seek Him only when we have a problem or in time of need. I encourage you to incorporate your faith into your daily life; it will help you be successful.

Let me share with you an example of how I used my faith in the workplace.

An employee was not a good fit for our organization and was clearly unhappy. I had to fire him. I could have "documented" him out of the organization. However, I felt that it would serve no good purpose and it would cause a great deal of ill will.

I informed my boss that I was going to terminate this employee and I was going to do it in a Christian fashion, thereby creating no ill will. I called the employee into my office and discussed the matter with him. I did not put him on the defensive. I told him that the job was not a fit for his considerable talents and that we both knew that he would be far happier in another employment situation. Although he was terminated, I agreed to continue to pay his salary and medical insurance for another month. I would do whatever I could to help him get a new position, and I did. I also told him that I would not contest his unemployment benefit request if he sought it. Our meeting ended with a handshake.

In the short term these compassionate measures may have seemed costly to some, however, they prevented a frivolous lawsuit, instilled a large dose of good will, and enabled him to leave the office with his head held high. During the entire process, I told myself that I was going to handle this termination in a Christian fashion. I think I hit the mark.

The media and liberal politicians have tried to drive faith out of our public lives to the point that a student cannot give thanks to God in a high school commencement ceremony. This is ridiculous. I am including President Lincoln's Thanksgiving address of 1864 to demonstrate how this great man's faith in God helped him lead our nation. Those who are of the opinion that we need to keep faith out of the public square, need to read this address to realize how misguided they are.

A Proclamation of Thanksgiving

by Abraham Lincoln, President of the United States of America
on October 20, 1864[15]

It has pleased Almighty God to prolong our national life another year, defending us with his guardian care against unfriendly designs from abroad, and vouchsafing to us in His mercy many and signal victories over the enemy, who is of our own household. It has also pleased our Heavenly Father to favor as well our citizens in their homes as our soldiers in their camps and our sailors on the rivers and seas with unusual health. He has largely augmented our free population by emancipation and by immigration, while he has opened to us new sources of wealth, and has crowned the labor of our working men in every department of industry with abundant rewards. Moreover, He has been pleased to animate and inspire our minds and hearts with fortitude, courage and resolution sufficient for the great trial of civil war into which we have been brought by our adherence as a nation to the cause of Freedom and Humanity, and to afford to us reasonable hopes of an ultimate and happy deliverance from all our dangers and afflictions.

Now, therefore, I, Abraham Lincoln, President of the United States, do, hereby, appoint and set apart the last Thursday in November next as a day, which I desire to be observed by all my fellow-citizens wherever they may then be as a day of Thanksgiving and Praise to Almighty God the beneficent Creator and Ruler of the Universe. And I do farther recommend to my fellow-citizens aforesaid that on that occasion they do reverently humble themselves in the dust and from thence offer up penitent and fervent prayers and supplications to the Great Disposer of events for a return of the inestimable

---

[15]www.americanhistory.org

blessings of Peace, Union and Harmony throughout the land, which it has pleased him to assign as a dwelling place for ourselves and for our posterity throughout all generations.

In testimony whereof, I have hereunto set my hand and caused the seal of the United States to be affixed.

Consider This:

● *Let us hold fast the profession of our faith without wavering; (for he is faithful that promised;)*
　Hebrews 10:23

● *A faithful man shall abound with blessings...*
　Proverbs 28:20

● *He who has faith has... an inward reservoir of courage, hope, confidence, calmness, and assuring trust that all will come out well-even though to the world it may appear to come out most badly.*
　B.C. Forbes

● *Do you wait for extraordinary moments to practice your faith, or do you practice faith in the small things?*

Application:

● Pray that your faith will increase daily.
● Faith is confidence and assurance that things will turn out just fine. Faith will see you through adversity.
● Exercise faith to comfort a sick soul or a troubled conscience.
● God never gives up on you, so do not give up on Him!
● The greater your faith in God, the greater your accomplishments.

[The Biblical Perspective] *Faith*

The LORD shall preserve thee from all evil: he shall preserve thy soul. The LORD shall preserve thy going out and thy coming in from this time forth, and even for evermore.
Psalm 121:7-8

In hard times we are drawn to our faith. Daily life must have seemed a struggle to the ancient Israelites. Imagine living then without the modern conveniences and advances we have today. From healthcare to creature comforts, we live in a world vastly different from theirs. Yet the very essence of human existence is still the same. We have war, illness, struggles, and conflict. We can mitigate the pain to some degree, but we still suffer.

This Psalm shows God will guard His people from all evil. It was likely written by peoples living in the mountains, possibly Mount Zion, the site of the temple and safety. They knew the Lord would guard their souls then and forever. We must demonstrate the same faith and know that when things go wrong at work or at home, our struggles are minor compared to the big picture. As a Christian, God will protect your soul and you are assured of eternal life.

Like the ancient people of Israel who had faith in God, we must access that huge reservoir of faith to successfully meet our daily challenges head on. While we may not be doing battle with the Philistines, we are battling the corrosive and corrupting influences of our modern culture each day. We need to put our faith in God, seek His wisdom, and follow his teachings in the Bible. We will be the better for it.

Use your faith as a coat of armor to shield you. Moses' faith freed a nation; David's faith slew a giant; Paul's faith was indomitable; your faith can move mountains. Nothing is as assuring and comforting as knowing that your life rests in God's hands. Have faith and move boldly toward your life's calling.

Guest Commentary

On Faith
by Jerry Coffee
U.S. Navy Captain, Retired

I was a POW in the communist prisons of North Vietnam for over seven years. Faith was the key to my survival; primarily faith in my God. Emanating from that foundation was faith in myself, faith in my family and comrades, and faith in my country, America. More importantly, after my repatriation, I found that these four aspects of faith have continued to serve me well on a daily basis.

For example, faith in one's self, derives from the ability to fathom the events of September 11, 2001-the date that changed everything. Faith in ourselves requires that we not just cope with such change, but understand the inevitability of change. We need to prepare ourselves for whatever changes may come, embrace them, and make them work in our favor. Let us have faith in ourselves, plant our feet firmly with finality, and state unequivocally: "This is right and that is wrong; this is moral and that is immoral; this is good and that is evil; and I know the difference!" Faith in ourselves means not becoming POWs – "Prisoners of Woe" (as in "Woe is me!") – while wishing we were somewhere else, doing something else, or wishing this or that hadn't happened. We need to play the cards we are dealt.

Faith in one another, embodied in our prison motto, "Unity Over Self," applies equally to our family unit and to our corporate organization. Unity is dependent upon communication, which, in prison, was accomplished mostly by tapping on the walls from cell to cell. On a daily basis, open and honest communication based upon faith in one another is essential in solving our mutual problems and in forming partnerships essential to our success.

Unfortunately, modern technology makes face-to-face communication too rare, which frequently makes understanding and empathy more difficult, almost as if we were tapping through walls. Faith in one another means trusting one another and giving the benefit of the doubt, at least until the other gives reason not to trust.

In Hanoi, we were bombarded with anti-American propaganda each day; negative information about the war, our society, our free enterprise system, our leadership. Like everything in a communist society-all were based upon lies, slander, and deceit. Sometimes keeping faith in America was difficult, but we did! Here at home the negativity and sensationalism of our mainstream media can have the same effect. It undermines our trust and confidence in our political system, our institutions, and our leadership. However, if we keep faith in our country and the principles and values upon which it was founded, then we will have the foundation to counteract the doubt and negativity heaped upon us by the media, and by those who have lost faith.

Another American there before me scratched two words on the wall of a cell: "God=Strength!" For me, that really worked. In spite of the solitary confinement, I was never ever totally alone and I could always find a little bit more strength when I needed it. We all had our own daily spiritual routines, but every Sunday morning the senior man in each cell block would pass a certain signal (called "Church Call") through the walls and every man who could stand did so. In some semblance of togetherness, we recited the pledge of allegiance to our flag, the Lord's Prayer, and frequently, the twenty-third Psalm. Those years in prison taught me that we could not educate our children, legislate our laws, conduct our businesses, or defend our country in a spiritual vacuum. Faith in our God is the foundation for all faith; our belief in things unseen; the opposite of fear; the last line of defense.

Through faith, we can overcome any obstacle, achieve any goal, survive any ordeal, and that potential is already in each of us. Bob McDermott has written a valuable guide to these principles-which can be the foundation for personal success, fulfillment, and triumph. And I would suggest that faith comes before all the rest.

In hard times
we are drawn to our faith
to successfully meet our daily
challenges head on and move
boldly toward your life's calling.

[Principle Sixteen]
Compassion

Hereby perceive we the love of God, because he laid down his life for us: and we ought to lay down our lives for the brethren. But whoso hath this world's good, and seeth his brother have need, and shutteth up his bowels of compassion from him, how dwelleth the love of God in him? My little children, let us not love in word, neither in tongue; but in deed and in truth.

1 John 3:16-18

Every time I see a homeless person on the street asking for money, my first reaction is to reach in my pocket. I was not always that way, but I am now. Some people might think that I'm enabling the alcoholic or the drug addict in their behavior. I believe that when people have reached the point in their lives where they are begging for money on the street, I need to have compassion and not judge them. I am reminded of the Jim Carrey movie, *Bruce Almighty*, when a homeless person turns out to be Jesus himself. We should not be hasty in judging others, but we should be hasty in showing compassion.

During the past year, my wife and I have learned a huge lesson in compassion. We wanted to raise another child, but due to medical reasons were not able to bear more children. When we heard that a little baby boy needed a home, we jumped at the chance.

We let the child welfare agency know that we were a willing family and that we had already gone through foster training. In a matter of days, after the background check and interview, we were thrilled to receive our little blessing. Mattogofie means "wonderful" in Samoan and he is half-Samoan and half Hawaiian. It had been fourteen years since we had an infant in the home, so I was a little rusty, but in a few days I got the hang of caring for a newborn again.

From the beginning, our intentions were to adopt this boy and we made it clear to all concerned. About three weeks after we had little "Matta" in our care, the social worker came to visit. Social Services had done some more checking on us and found out some good things. The social worker asked us if we would consider bringing in little Matta's three siblings. They were not being properly cared for and needed to be moved immediately. These siblings had never lived with Matta because he was removed from the hospital after authorities learned that was an "ice baby" (a child exposed to crystal methamphetamine in the uterus).

The social worker made it clear to us that the older siblings were not up for adoption and our care would be only temporary. My wife and I considered the social worker's request for several days. Bringing in three additional children, plus the infant was going to be a huge amount of work. However, after much prayer and consideration, we agreed to have Matta's siblings in our home.

We took the three older children to see their biological parents and we took them to dental and medical checkups. Things were going along fairly well until one day I asked the social worker about Matta's adoption proceedings. Specifically, I wanted to know when the state was going to move forward. She started to hem and haw... this was the first sign of real trouble.

By agreeing to provide foster care for the other siblings, we had unified the children for the first time and our adoption opportunity became muddied. Since the kids were together and thriving, the social worker saw no need to rush the adoption proceedings and give us custody of baby Matta. It seemed that we were being penalized for caring for the three older siblings. This was very troubling to my wife and me. It became apparent that we couldn't just adopt Matta; we would have to agree to adopt all four of them! It was now a package deal. This is not what was originally presented to us and not what we expected. At the same time, their biological parents were not making adequate progress on their road to recovery and sobriety. All of this made the prospect of adopting all four children very real.

My wife worried about how the children would react to her when they got older. The three oldest children knew their parents and had weekly visits with them. My wife did not want to get burned emotionally. I shared her concerns with the social worker and told her that my wife was hesitant about outright adoption of the older siblings, but that we would be glad to care for them as guardians.

Apparently, the social worker believed that we would return the three older children to the state social services agency after we finalized the adoption of the baby. After over a year in our care, we learned that the social worker was trying to place all of the children with a grandmother on another island. When we heard this we were flabbergasted! However, all of this turmoil with the social worker had a silver lining. It made us really appreciate how much these children meant to us. The very thought of them leaving was heartbreaking.

Thankfully, because of the social worker's actions, my wife abandoned all hesitation toward adopting all the children. We became a fully united team and were determined. We hired a lawyer to adopt these children. As of this writing, we have encumbered $25,000 in legal fees and we still have not completed the process.

We have gone through a tremendous amount of emotional turmoil due to our desire to provide these children with a good and loving home. That being said, my wife and I have been so blessed since we took these children into our home. I believe God has blessed us for displaying compassion to these little ones. God has been showing us His favor. We have been blessed emotionally, financially, spiritually, and in every way.

Consider This:

● *Put on therefore, as the elect of God, holy and beloved, bowels of mercies, kindness, humbleness of mind, meekness, longsuffering...*

Colossians 3:12

● *Blessed are the merciful: for they shall obtain mercy. Blessed are the pure in heart: for they shall see God.*

Matthew 5:7-8

● *What this world needs is a new kind of army-the army of the kind.*

Cleveland Amory

● *When you see a person asking for money on the street, do you judge that individual, or do you share your financial blessings with them?*

In 1987, my wife and I were living with her cousin George. He was a few years older than us, but in the same boat financially. He needed to share the cost of an apartment, like we did, with extended family. Therefore, we all chipped in and got an apartment together.

George was a kind man. I really liked him. One Saturday morning, I woke up and walked into the kitchen. From there, I could see the living room area and I saw what appeared to be a young woman sleeping on the couch. I immediately went back to my room and woke my wife. She told me that the "woman" was Tommy, George's brother. Tommy was a transvestite and went by the name "Leilani." Tommy needed a place to stay and George was his brother and both were my wife's cousins. In Samoan culture, the extended ed family is considered immediate family and treated as such. You never turn away your family; that is compassion.

Tommy looked like a woman-enough to convince me at first glance. He took female steroids to soften his appearance and he even had breast tissue. His face had no trace of facial hair and he dieted to maintain a very slight and petite frame. He dressed in female clothing, cinching his belt tightly around his waist, to give himself an hourglass female shape.

Tommy lived with us for several months. Although I disagreed with Tommy's lifestyle choice, forever objected to having him in the home, I never bothered or harassed him about his behavior. We were young and had only an infant at the time so there really was no issue with influencing our children. One time I asked him why he chose to live the way he was living and why he continued to take female hormones. He seemed offended by my questions. After that, we didn't talk about it.

When Tommy would go to a bar, young military men under the influence of booze were easily fooled by his true gender. One time, a young sailor called the home and asked for Leilani. I handed the phone to Tommy and he answered the call in his feminine voice. He made a date with the young man. I told his brother George and we were both concerned that Tommy was going to get hurt by pretending to be a woman. George talked to Tommy about his behavior, but it didn't seem to make a difference.

In early 1988, my wife and I moved out of the apartment. I went back into the Marine Corps, while my wife went to live with her parents. We returned to Hawaii in 1992. A year or so later I was watching the news and saw this headline: "Schofield Solider Arrested for Murder of a Prostitute." George's worst dreams had come true. Poor Tommy had turned to prostitution parading as a woman outside of Schofield Barracks. Apparently, a solider discovered that Tommy was not a woman and he beat him to death. This was not a premeditated case of murder, the man just snapped. It was a tragically sad story. Two lives were ruined and I couldn't help but to feel compassion for both Tommy and the soldier.

As much as I disagreed with Tommy' choices, I could not turn my wife's cousin out on the streets. We can have compassion and pray for our fellow man to repent while strongly disagreeing with their chosen lifestyle.

Consider This:

● *But the mercy of the LORD is from everlasting to everlasting upon them that fear him, and his righteousness unto children's children...*

Psalm 103:17

● *Kindness is the language which the deaf can hear and the blind can see.*

Mark Twain

● *How would you handle a loved one who has made poor choices? Would you ostracize that person, or offer compassion?*

When my wife and I got married in 1987, I embraced her family and her culture. They are a wonderful and loving people. We moved away from Hawaii after I was commissioned into the Marine Corps.

In Hawaii, we are fortunate to enjoy the American culture-in addition to interacting with diverse ethnic groups that came here to work in the plantations generations ago. After several years on the mainland, I wanted to return home to Hawaii. I wanted our children to fully embrace their Samoan heritage and be exposed to the richness of Hawaii's multicultural society.

I am more secure in who I am and can now fully accept my wife's Samoan culture. On occasion, this requires some tolerance. For example, at weddings my wife is expected to give gifts to the bride and groom. Gifts are also presented to families of the deceased at funerals. These events can sometimes require her to be gone for several hours for two or three consecutive nights. She enjoys attending these events because she is helping her parents and is carrying on her cultural traditions. When we moved back, I knew that she would be required to participate in these events. I also knew that if I wanted to make her happy, I needed to tolerate these infrequent instances.

My wife and I decided that we wanted to help her parents. We asked them to move in with us. This raised their standard of living, while placing additional demands on our family. She welcomed these responsibilities as a good Samoan daughter.

Consequently, when her family comes to Hawaii for a visit, we often serve as the host. This can really cramp one's style. Last summer we had twenty-two people in our home for about a week. People slept everywhere. I found this to be a bit much, but my wife was happy to accommodate her family. In fact, she was more than happy--she was overjoyed and ecstatic!

Our children have grown up watching all of this. They look at their mom as an example of someone who is a giver. I am proud to say that they are turning out to be compassionate and unselfish people. They understand and embrace their Samoan heritage. Someday, I hope they will look back and appreciate the compassion I have shown to their mother's side of the family.

Consider This:

● *Though I speak with the tongues of men and of angels, and have not charity, I am become as sounding brass, or a tinkling cymbal. And though I have the gift of prophecy, and understand all mysteries, and all knowledge; and though I have all faith, so that I could remove mountains, and have not charity, I am nothing.*

 I Corinthians. 13:1-3

● *Never apologize for showing feeling. When you do so, you apologize for the truth.*

 Benjamin Disraeli

● *Would your family say that you are compassionate to their needs, desires, and wants?*

Walter A. Dods, Jr., had a distinguished thirty-six year career at First Hawaiian Bank where he began as director of advertising and public relations. He worked his way through management in every part of the bank, and was named its president at forty-three years of age, making him one of the youngest presidents in the nation for an institution of its size. In 2004, he retired as its chairman and chief executive officer.

Walter Dods rose from modest means to help a whole community. Under his compassionate leadership, the bank was always active in contributing to local charities. He led the way by giving his time, talent, and personal wealth. His spirit of charity was contagious-reaching all the way down to the teller level. This is the type of compassionate leadership that we should all emulate.

I met with Mr. Dods in his office twice. During one of those meetings, he shared how his tellers were among the highest per capita donors to the Aloha United Way, which raises money and distributes them to many local charitable organizations in the state. He was extremely proud of these hardworking employees who donated substantial sums from their modest paychecks. Moreover, most of his senior executive staff spent so much time volunteering for boards and other charitable organizations that it was often a challenge to get them to focus on their banking jobs. It was not a criticism on his part, but an observation.

Mr. Dods has often been mentioned as a potential political candidate in our state. He would have the overwhelming support of the community because of all of the charitable work he has done over the years, regardless of his political party affiliation.

Remarkably, Mr. Dods shuns the spotlight. He does not seek media coverage or recognition for his charitable works. He just does them.

One of his lasting legacies will be the Hawaii Open PGA golf tournament.

Each year this tournament is used as a vehicle to raise hundreds of thousands of dollars for local charities and good causes. It would not exist without the commitment and sponsorship of First Hawaiian Bank. Mr. Dods knows the true definition of compassion and caring for his fellow man.

When Jesus was asked what the greatest commandment was, He told the people to love God with all their heart. The second greatest commandment is to love your neighbor as yourself. Compassion is unconditional love for others.

I like to say that compassion is no ordinary word. Compassion calls us to action through our love for Jesus Christ. When we exercise compassion toward our fellow man, we are at our best-infused with the spirit of Christ.

Consider This:

● *But thou, O Lord, art a God full of compassion, and gracious, long suffering, and plenteous in mercy and truth.*

Psalm 86:15

● *How far you go in life depends on your being tender with the young, compassionate with the aged, sympathetic with the striving and tolerant of the weak and strong. Because someday in life you will have been all of these.*

George Washington Carver

● *Do you live out your faith by showing compassion for others and loving your neighbor as yourself? If so, how?*

Application:
● Display compassion toward the sick.
● Exercise compassion towards the down trodden, homeless, and
  the hopeless.

- Give the panhandler a couple of dollars. Let them know you care.
- Volunteer at a charity or non-profit organization that helps others in need.
- Give back to your community by being generous in donations to your chosen causes.
- Display compassion to a fallen foe, offering help when in need.
- Don't forget those closest to us. Show compassion to family members.
- Demonstrate compassion toward co-workers who seem to be having a tough time.
- Have compassion for our youth and mentor them when possible.

[The Biblical Perspective] *Compassion*

And again he entered into Capernaum after some days; and it was noised that he was in the house. And straightway many were gathered together, insomuch that there was no room to receive them, no, not so much as about the door: and he preached the word unto them. And they come unto him, bringing one sick of the palsy, which was borne of four. And when they could not come nigh unto him for the press, they uncovered the roof where he was: and when they had broken it up, they let down the bed wherein the sick of the palsy lay. When Jesus saw their faith, he said unto the sick of the palsy, Son, thy sins be forgiven thee. I say unto thee, Arise, and take up thy bed, and go thy way into thine house. And immediately he arose, took up the bed, and went forth before them all; insomuch that they were all amazed, and glorified God, saying, We never saw it on this fashion.

Mark 2:1-5, 11-12

Charity and compassion are another word for love. It is the act of helping those less fortunate, the downtrodden, the disenfranchised, and the helpless. We are called to help those who are in need.

In the story above, a man had palsy and had been paralyzed for many years.

Jesus was in town and they had faith that He could heal their helpless friend. The four friends carried the man with palsy on a mat, but they couldn't get pass the door due to the crowd. However, they didn't give up. Can you imagine what it took for them to carry their paralyzed friend up to the roof of the house, break open the roof with a large hole, and then carefully lower him on the mat into the room below. Jesus was moved by the faith of the man's friends. "When Jesus saw their faith," He forgave the man's sins and healed him. The man arose and everyone was amazed and glorified God. By their actions, the man's friends demonstrated faith and compassion. In turn, they were also blessed.

Like this man's friends, we may be called to go to great lengths to provide comfort to our family members in their time of trouble. It may a great inconvenience, but we share our concern and love for that person by just showing up. Compassion is a must in order to help our loved ones through the healing process. And they will never forget our kindness.

Jesus had compassion and exercised charity for all of humankind, by sacrificing His own life on the cross for our sins. He did not have to do it, but He was called to do it because He was the very definition of love. In life, we must strive to display compassion, emulating the example of Christ.

When I was young, I used to ridicule the panhandlers. I called them bums and said other unkind things. I'd put them down and tell them to get a job, but I never gave them money. I had no compassion for the less fortunate.

Now I have empathy for people who are so down and out that they are willing to stand on a street corner and humiliate themselves by begging for money. Who am I to deny them a couple of bucks? Once I give them that gift of love, it is up to them how they use it.

You never know what human disguise Jesus might be wearing. Remember, He told us to treat the least of our brothers as He would treat us. I really try and practice this. Help those in need with your time, talent, and treasure. You might just be helping Jesus Himself.

For I was an hungered, and ye gave me meat: I was thirsty, and ye gave me drink: I was a stranger, and ye took me in: Naked, and ye clothed me: I was sick, and ye visited me: I was in prison, and ye came unto me.

Then shall the righteous answer him, saying, Lord, when saw we thee an hungered, and fed thee? or thirsty, and gave thee drink? When saw we thee a stranger, and took thee in? or naked, and clothed thee? Or when saw we thee sick, or in prison, and came unto thee? And the King shall answer and say unto them, Verily I say unto you, Inasmuch as ye have done it unto one of the least of these my brethren, ye have done it unto me.

Matthew 25:35-40

Guest Commentary

Compassionate Man

By Dr. Leon Watson, PhD
Scholar, Mentor

My father was a tough ghetto street kid from Detroit, with an alcoholic father, a mom who boogied off to Broadway to be an actress. As a kid he sold ice door-to-door. He boxed to survive, and he came up through the factory unions in the 1930s-70s. Mom was always her own person, and lived with an open door and heart. Both were as compassionate as they knew how. However, both had serious issues of their own. These of course colored my viewpoint of life and limited or uncorked my options. I learned to be cute, to hide when necessary, and to get out on my own early.

I went to college and got lots of degrees. I eventually did many things, often working two or three jobs at the same time. I paid my way everywhere and in many exotic places in the world. I had exciting times working on many interesting projects.

It meant being strong enough to survive; perceptive enough to take advantage of the options; and willing to live with strange situations. Sometimes it meant just showing up with some integrity.

At first, this had little to do with being compassionate or caring. Compassion generally sounded like a good idea to me. You make good friends; you help people. Most girls like it, too. The harder question for me was why? Granted, being compassionate has a survival value, and can be noble, and even rewarding. But I wondered if compassion had a higher purpose. Why should I bother?

I eventually realized that I was one of the billions of men who really did not care about those people you see on gossip magazine covers. Why should I care who the sexiest person is, or who has the messiest divorce, or who the richest person is? Lately I am having a hard time with fragmentation of our nation into selfish little neo-tribes with designer artifacts and media pleasing pseudo-cultures. They ask me to care about their differences, their pitiful idolized existences, and their ninny spectrum. I can't. They are artificial.

I have found people to care about. Real people. They are all around me. They teach me to be compassionate, and have been so with me more times than I could ever remember.

Let me tell you about the treasures I have found. Lost boys have become my sons --we went fishing, and played basketball, and yelled and punched each other. Lost girls have become my daughters--we talked about their shattered hopes, and threw flower petals in the water. Lost people have become my friends. And a lost man has become me. God is compassionate with us all, but we have to share the pain to get the joy. It is a long and wonderful story that is still unfolding, including a lot of messy stuff that doesn't make much sense at any given time.

So if you ask me about the essence of compassion, I would say to choose wisely in the face of plenty. It helps if you can lose it all and yourself for a while. Then eventually find somebody, and show up in someone's life. Just show up. Do whatever you can. Be inconveniently available. Often, that is enough. Wrap your arms around wounded kids, women or men, or whoever is handy. They will often do it back. (God really does it all anyway.)

[Affirmation]
Practice Makes Perfect

In this book, we have discussed many topics. I have tried to use stories, mostly from my own experience to amplify the Biblical principles of success. Most of these principles can be found in other secular manuscripts. However, I wanted the readers to know that these principles were not my own made up personal philosophy, nor was I some new age guru. I just wanted to reach out to this generation they way others have in the past and say - Here is the way to go if you want to live a richer and fuller life.

Too often, we sit in church and the sermon goes over our head... it does not resonate. I cannot tell you how many times I heard the parable about reaping and sowing and it just went right by me. Part of the equation is that you have to be ready to receive the information, and if you are reading this, you are there now. The second part of the equation is searching and then having someone point out that the answer was in front of you all along. I hope I have helped you discover the obvious, that the Bible is the greatest handbook for success and general guide to living that has ever been produced.

It is not rocket science but age old wisdom. As the old saying goes, there is no new idea under the sun, and so it is.

I have used these principles in my own life on a daily basis. They work. I find that I am most happy when just concentrating on implementing these principles when dealing with others. The journey of getting this book published and creating this program have sometimes sidetracked even me from focusing on what is really important in life, which is living a life of faith, one that is guided by a deep and abiding love of God. With God, we can accomplish anything. Using the principles and tools in this book provides, you are given a general methodology for those who want to be successful in this world. The world may change, but the principles do not.

No matter what adversity or challenge you may face you can be successful. In closing, I leave you with these words:

"If God be for us, who can be against us?"